AN EVENT-BASED SCIENCE MODULE

EARTHQUAKE!

STUDENT EDITION

Russell G. Wright

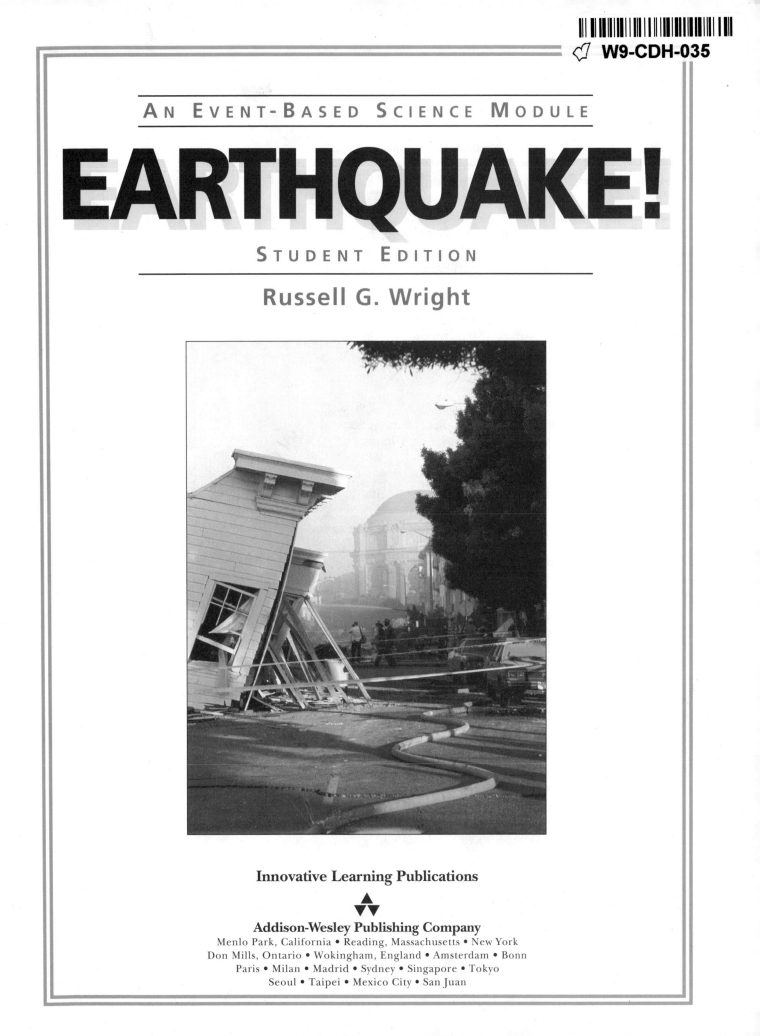

Innovative Learning Publications

Addison-Wesley Publishing Company

Menlo Park, California • Reading, Massachusetts • New York
Don Mills, Ontario • Wokingham, England • Amsterdam • Bonn
Paris • Milan • Madrid • Sydney • Singapore • Tokyo
Seoul • Taipei • Mexico City • San Juan

The developers of Event-Based Science have been encouraged and supported at every step in the creative process by the Superintendent and Board of Education of Montgomery County Public Schools, Rockville, Maryland (MCPS). The superintendent and board are committed to the systemic improvement of science instruction, grades preK–12. EBS is one of many projects undertaken to ensure the scientific literacy of *all* students.

Montgomery County Public Schools

The developers of *Earthquake!* pay special tribute to the editors, publisher, and reporters of *USA Today*. Without their cooperation and support the creation of this module would not have been possible.

Photographs: Cover Ed Kashi, Gamma Liaison; pages 2, 5, 8, 12, 17, 22, 23, 29, and 40 United States Geological Survey; pages 4 and 34 *USA Today*; all "Student Voices" Nancy Ermoian.
Managing Editor: Cathy Anderson
Project Editor: Katarina Stenstedt
Production/Manufacturing Coordinator: Leanne Collins
Design Manager: Jeff Kelly
Text and Cover Design: Frank Loose Design, Portland, Oregon

This book is published by Innovative Learning Publications™, an imprint of the Alternative Publishing Group of Addison-Wesley Publishing Company.

This material is based upon work supported by the National Science Foundation under grant number MDR-9154094. Any opinions, findings, conclusions, or recommendations expressed in this publication are those of the Event-Based Science Project and do not necessarily reflect the views of the National Science Foundation.

9 10-DR-99

Contents

Preface

The Event-Based Science Model

Earthquake! is an earth-science unit that follows the Event-Based Science (EBS) Instructional Model. You will watch "live" television news coverage of the World Series earthquake of 1989 and read *USA Today* reports about it. Your discussions about the earthquake will show you and your teacher that you already know a lot about earth-science concepts involved in the event. Next, a real-world task puts you and your classmates in the roles of people who must use scientific knowledge and processes to solve a problem related to earthquakes. You will probably need more information before you start the task. If you do, *Earthquake!* provides hands-on activities and a variety of reading material to give you some of the background you need. About halfway through the unit, you will be ready to begin the task. Your teacher will assign you a role to play and turn you and your team loose to complete the task. You will spend the rest of the time in this unit working on that task.

Scientific Literacy

Today, a literate citizen is expected to know more than how to read, write, and do simple arithmetic. Today, literacy includes knowing how to analyze problems, ask critical questions, and explain events. A literate citizen must also be able to apply scientific knowledge and processes to new situations. Event-Based Science allows you to practice these skills by placing the study of science in a meaningful context.

Knowledge cannot be transferred to your mind from the mind of your teacher, or from the pages of a textbook. Nor can knowledge occur in isolation from the other things you know about and have experienced in the real world. The Event-Based Science model is based on the idea that the best way to learn something is to be actively engaged in it.

Therefore, the Event-Based Science model simulates real-life events and experiences to make your learning more authentic and memorable. First, the event is brought to life through television news coverage. Viewing the news allows you to be there "as it happens," and that is as close as you can get to actually experiencing the event. Second, by simulating the kinds of teamwork and problem solving that occur every day in our work places and communities, you will experience the role that scientific knowledge and teamwork play in the lives of ordinary people. Thus *Earthquake!* is built around simulations of real-life events and experiences that affected people's lives and environments dramatically.

In an Event-Based Science classroom, you become the workers, your product is a solution to a real problem, and your teacher is your coach, guide, and advisor. You will be assessed on how you use scientific processes and concepts to solve problems as well as on the quality of your work.

One of the primary goals of the EBS Project is to place the learning of science in a real-world context and to make the learning of science fun. You should not allow yourself to become frustrated. If you cannot find a specific piece of information, it is okay to be creative. For example, if you are working as the economist for your team and you cannot find the kinds of industries that are located in the community you are investigating, use your imagination, but keep it realistic. Base your response on the real places and things you know about. Just remember to identify your creations as fictional.

Student Resources

Earthquake! is unlike a regular textbook. An Event-Based Science module tells a story about a real event; it has real newspaper articles about the event, and features that explain the scientific concepts involved in the event. It also contains laboratory investigations for you to conduct in your science class, and activities that you may do in English, math, social studies, or technology education classes. In addition, an Event-Based Science module gives you and your classmates a real-world task to do. The task is always done by teams of students, with each team member performing a real-life role while completing an important part of the task. The task cannot be completed without you and everyone else on your team doing their parts. The team approach allows you to share your knowledge and strengths. It also helps you learn to work with a team in a real-world situation. Today, most professionals work in teams.

Interviews with people who actually serve in the roles you are playing are scattered throughout the Event-Based Science module. Students who actually experienced the event tell their stories throughout the module too.

Since this module is unlike a regular textbook, you have much more flexibility in using it.

- You may read **The Story** for enjoyment or to find clues that will help you tackle your part of the task.

- You may read selections from the **Discovery File** when you need help understanding something in the story or when you need help with the task.

- You may read all the **On the Job** features because you are curious about what professionals do, or you may read only the interview with the professional who works in the role you've chosen because it may give you ideas that will help you complete the task.

- You may read the **In the News** features because they catch your eye, or as part of your search for information.

- You will probably read all the **Student Voices** features because they are interesting stories told by middle-school students like yourself.

Earthquake! is also unlike regular textbooks in that the collection of resources found in it is not meant to be complete. You must find additional information from other sources, too. Textbooks, encyclopedias, pamphlets, magazine and newspaper articles, videos, films, filmstrips, computer databases, and people in your community are all potential sources of useful information. It is vital to your preparation as a scientifically literate citizen of the twenty-first century that you get used to finding information on your own.

The shape of a new form of science education is beginning to emerge, and the Event-Based Science Project is leading the way. We hope you enjoy your experience with this module as much as we enjoyed developing it.

—Russell G. Wright, Ed.D.
Project Director and Principal Author

An Encounter with Our Restless Earth

Sitting in the stands of Candlestick Park stadium in San Francisco, California, on a cool October day, some 60,000 baseball fans eagerly awaited the start of the third game in the World Series. Little did they know that a "geological umpire" would call off the game just minutes later.

In the neighboring Santa Cruz Mountains, 50 miles (80 kilometers) away, two segments of the earth called *plates* gave way to nature's own squeeze play. Over 11 miles below a mountain peak called Loma Prieta (pronounced "low-ma pre-et-ah"), one plate moved upward and to the northwest about 75 inches, while the other plate shot 51 inches to the southeast. The result?

That violent release of energy on October 17, 1989, at 5:04 p.m. pacific daylight time, caused a train of vibrations to roar through the earth. Waves of energy rippled outward from the edge of the shifting plates at more than one mile per second. Across the globe, jiggling seismometers eavesdropped, in one sense, on a disaster in the making.

In less than 15 seconds, thousands of landslides covered roads. More than 400 single-family homes were destroyed and 18,306 residences were structurally damaged; 97 businesses and 3 public buildings were also destroyed. Falling debris, toppled buildings, and collapsing freeways injured 3,757 people and took the lives of 67.

Basic services, such as gas, electricity, and telephone, were immediately disrupted, affecting about a million people. Many of the operating telephone circuits were jammed as thousands of callers sought information about the damage inflicted by the rolling earthquake.

The most deadly result of the shifting earth occurred when tons of concrete from the top deck of Oakland's double-deck Nimitz Freeway—built in the 1950s—fell onto the four lower lanes of road, crushing 41 motorists to death. A section of the San Francisco–Oakland Bay Bridge also fell from the upper deck onto the lower deck, killing one person. In this instance, earthquake-resistant joints installed in 1976 kept this bridge largely intact.

Another known hazard that sustained major damage was an area of San Francisco called the Marina District. Built over a landfill of sand and rubble, 200 buildings were structurally damaged when the sandy soil became the consistency of a dense fluid because of the rapidly shaking ground.

The Candlestick Park grandstand, filled with World Series spectators, swayed back and forth with the ground tremors. While the stadium's structure and foundation suffered only minor damage under the stress and strain of the shaking ground, television transmis-

STUDENT VOICES

I was outside at my house playing basketball, and my dad was working on the car. I realized we were having an earthquake when my dog started barking. I shot the basketball, and the rim moved. I ran inside and took cover under a doorway. After the earthquake, it was cold, and it was hard to do anything because there was no light. It was also scary.

JONATHON DOMINGUEZ
SALINAS, CALIFORNIA

➤ continued on page 2

Waverly Person, Geophysicist, Chief of the National Earthquake Information Center.

▶ continued from page 1

sions to baseball viewers outside the San Francisco stadium turned to static.

The World Series game was postponed and dazed fans tried to make their way home. Some fans later learned firsthand of the destruction caused by the earthquake when they returned to their destroyed homes. Others tuned in to radio and television reports to hear and watch details of the disaster unfold. ■

Discussion Questions:

- What is an earthquake?

- What causes earthquakes?

- Do earthquakes happen here?

- If an earthquake happened here, are we safe in this building?

- If an earthquake started now, what should you do?

- Have you ever experienced an earthquake? If so, describe what it felt like.

Killer quake jolts the Bay Area

By Judy Keen
USA TODAY

A violent earthquake devastated northern California Tuesday, killing more than 250 and injuring at least 400 others.

Tuesday night, as the death toll mounted hourly, the air was clogged with smoke from erupting fires, National Guardsmen patrolled to prevent looting, stranded people desperately hunted for their families and the USA tuned in to the unfolding disaster on TV.

The 15-second quake, which hit at 5:04 p.m. PDT, terrified 60,000 World Series fans in a swaying Candlestick Park. Game 3 was postponed.

"It felt like one of those monsters from a Japanese horror movie grabbed the building, shaking the ··· out of it," said San Jose's Margie Cornehl.

Today is critical: There's a chance of an even larger quake in the first 24 hours after a major temblor. Five strong aftershocks hit Tuesday night.

Experts say the area should brace for landslides and fires.

Dennis Redmond in San Francisco was in the same scary position as most people Tuesday: without power, light, water — and information. "The worst part is no one knows what's going on."

As many as 200 died when a mile-long portion of I-880 in Oakland collapsed; at least six died in Santa Cruz, just 10 miles from the quake's epicenter; six more in the flattening of a San Francisco apartment building;

and at least one on the Bay Bridge after a 30-foot section of the upper deck caved in.

The quake registered 6.9 on the Richter scale — a major quake — and the worst since the 1906 San Francisco earthquake, estimated at 8.3.

The Richter scale measures ground motion; each one-digit increase means a tenfold increase in magnitude.

The quake's center was on a segment of the San Andreas Fault where stress had built up, said Lisa Wald, a U.S. Geological Survey seismologist.

Tremors were felt 800 miles away in Los Angeles.

Damage was nightmarish:

▶ Fire blazed in San Francisco's Marina District and on the campus of the University of California at Berkeley.

▶ Most of the bridges connecting San Francisco to its suburbs were closed for inspection; the famous Golden Gate Bridge was undamaged.

▶ Up to 1 million customers lost electricity. Gas and phone service was also cut.

▶ Buildings, Highway 101 bridge collapsed in Hollister.

▶ The Diablo Canyon nuclear plant on the San Andreas fault near San Francisco was on alert to check for damage.

Officials wasted no time:

▶ The Army Corps of Engineers, called in to repair the Bay Bridge, said it would be repaired later this week.

▶ Gov. George Deukmejian cut short a trade mission to Frankfurt, West Germany.

USA TODAY, 18 OCTOBER 1989

Candlestick Park holds on

Candlestick Park opened in 1960 with seating for 42,500. Twelve years later, construction to enclose the stadium was completed, increasing seating to 58,000 for baseball. After a 1983 study warned that the upper deck canopy could collapse in an earthquake, renovations were done. How Tuesday's earthquake affected the stadium:

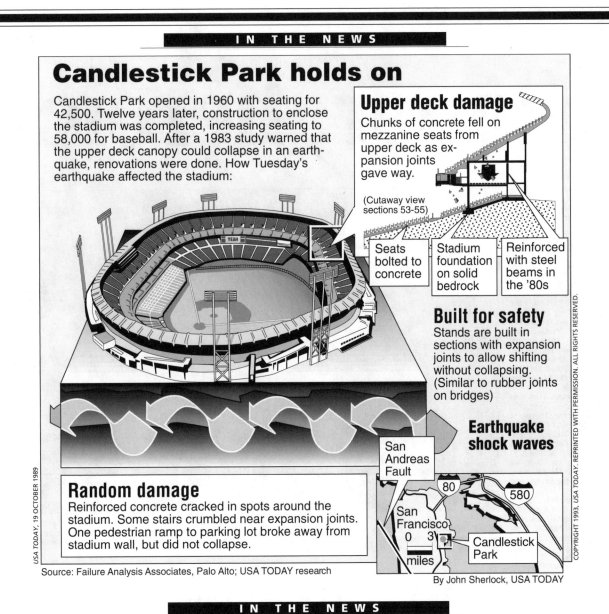

Upper deck damage

Chunks of concrete fell on mezzanine seats from upper deck as expansion joints gave way.

(Cutaway view sections 53-55)

Seats bolted to concrete

Stadium foundation on solid bedrock

Reinforced with steel beams in the '80s

Built for safety

Stands are built in sections with expansion joints to allow shifting without collapsing. (Similar to rubber joints on bridges)

Earthquake shock waves

San Andreas Fault

San Francisco

80   580

0   3

miles

Candlestick Park

Random damage

Reinforced concrete cracked in spots around the stadium. Some stairs crumbled near expansion joints. One pedestrian ramp to parking lot broke away from stadium wall, but did not collapse.

Source: Failure Analysis Associates, Palo Alto; USA TODAY research

By John Sherlock, USA TODAY

USA TODAY, 19 OCTOBER 1989

Utility crews say repairs within reach

By Steve Marshall
USA TODAY

Beneath quake-damaged Bay Area roads, there's plenty of activity for harried crews working to restore utility services.

"We were pretty lucky considering the size of the quake," says Tom Dickerman of San Francisco's water department. Time for repairs: "A day or so."

Work on utility lines is going on around the clock. Here's what's happening:

▶ **Water:** In Oakland, the water and sewer systems are fine, officials say. The water system serves 1.1 million in 317 square miles.

Waste-water treatment serves 600,000 customers.

In the district's northwest sector, a 3-foot break in a 60-inch water main will take up to a week to repair.

Seven communities on that main are getting water from a smaller one and residents are asked to conserve.

▶ **Electric:** Pacific Gas & Electric Co. brought in outside crews to help restore power to 400,000 customers still in the dark.

Hardest hit areas are close to the quake epicenter — Santa Cruz, Los Gatos, Watsonville and Hollister — as well as San Francisco.

▶ **Gas:** About 60,000 PG&E gas customers are without service; some shut off their own gas to stop leaks after the quake.

"We're working as swiftly as safety will allow," says Greg Pruett of PG&E. "We know of the tremendous inconvenience posed to our customers, but we just cannot restore service without being sure it's safe."

USA TODAY, 19 OCTOBER 1989

Humor, heroics

The question they will be asking for decades: "Where were you when the earthquake hit?" Here are some of the answers:

The cyclist

Don Laviletta says, "It was like bumper cars — only you could die in this game."

He was riding his motorcycle on the upper portion of the Bay Bridge.

"All of a sudden, it felt like I was driving on Jell-O. People started doing crazy things, veering all over the bridge, jumping out of cars.

"Cars were hitting the rails on the sides of the bridge and bouncing back in."

For a few seconds he was lucky. But then, "A lady in a big car swiped into me. I smashed into the ground and skidded to the side of the bridge; my helmet flew off. Cars just kept driving. I couldn't believe it."

Several cars ran over his $6,000 Yamaha. He just stood on the side of the bridge and watched.

"The last time I saw it, it was under the wheel of a stopped car, twisted beyond recognition. I keep thinking, that could've been me if I'd stayed with the bike."

Now Laviletta, 23, a technician in a psychiatric ward in Sonoma, lay on the floor at a Red Cross shelter. His right leg was in a splint. His face was bruised. The corner of his eye was covered with blood.

"This is it for me. I'm moving to Buffalo, N.Y., as soon as I can get out of this state. If I'm going to die, I don't want to die in an earthquake."

— Maria Goodavage

The rescuer

William McElroy was driving, not far from his home in Oakland, near the Nimitz Freeway, when the top deck collapsed.

McElroy, 52, wasn't hurt, but he could hear people moaning, crying for help. He decided to do what he could. He wasn't the only one.

The rescue workers were "poor people," McElroy said. "They came down from the projects with pliers, car jacks, wire cutters, flashlights and ladders" to help people out of their twisted cars. "We brought at least 12 or 13 on stretchers."

Most of the rescuers were black. The dazed and injured and dead were commuters, "100 percent white," McElroy said. But "in time of disaster, people don't ask your color. They just ask for help."

Usually, he said, "nobody gets much respect down here." That wasn't true Tuesday.

— Steve Sneddon

The immigrant

Ruby Magee was reminded of an earlier earthquake she never felt but which brought her to San Francisco.

After the 1906 quake, her father, James Currie, a building contractor in Perth, Australia, spread "the paper out on the front lawn and said to me, 'There's going to be a lot of work rebuilding that city.'"

A few days later they left for San Francisco.

Magee, now 94, remembers that for "four years, I passed block after block of burned homes. Only their blackened cellars remained."

This time, Magee's modest stucco home in San Jose escaped with minor damage: inch-wide cracks in her driveway, broken water pipes and shattered china.

Still, sitting in her living room when the quake hit, "I didn't have to wonder whether this was the big one. I knew it was the big one. . . . It was terrifying. . . . Everything came out of the cupboards. Even the refrigerator moved."

But she has no plans to leave. "California is the best place to live in the world. Earthquakes or not."

— Craig Sailor

The yuppie

Her Cuisinart tucked under her right arm, her bottle of Evian in her hand and a look of shock on her face, Maureen Brennan stood on a street corner in the exclusive Marina district on San Francisco Bay.

A few of her personal belongings — sweaters, skirts, shoes — were stacked on the cracked sidewalk. Her personal computer was next to a bag with the pork chops she had planned for a 6 p.m. dinner party Tuesday.

Instead, her apartment had come tumbling down. Her view of the Golden Gate Bridge was marred by the destruction.

The quake hit at 5:04 p.m. as Brennan was preparing dinner.

"I've got the pork chops in the bag," she said. "I hate to waste food."

It was one of the few laughs she could enjoy.

The volunteer

Bob Turek was headed to his new home from his new job when he noticed smoke around his block.

"I thought, 'Bummer. Some poor guy's house is on fire.' Then I realized it was mine."

After a spell of "hard luck," Turek, 37, recently found a telemarketing job at Time-Life Books. A week ago, he moved out of a shelter for the homeless into a $650-a-month one-bedroom apartment in the Marina district.

"I've always felt this was a very shaky building," she said of her three-story structure, which charges $1,000 a month for a one-bedroom unit. "I've always felt tremors here, even when they're far away."

A New York native who has lived by the bay about 10 years, she doesn't have earthquake insurance, she said. "It's too expensive."

— Carrie Muskat

USA TODAY, 19 OCTOBER 1989

By Tim Dillon, USA TODAY

HOME DESTROYED: Joan Miller, left, and Beth Roemer stand in front of their apartment building Wednesday in San Francisco's Marina district. The second floor of the building rests on the street. A fire fueled by gas destroyed a block of apartments in the district and forced the evacuation of many throughout the area.

amid the horror

But now flames were leaping through the roof of his apartment.

"It was completely engulfed. I just turned around and walked away. Why should I stand and watch my life literally go up in a puff of smoke?"

Turek, a San Francisco native, had no insurance. But then, he didn't have a lot to insure — a TV, radio, a bed and his clothes.

Now, he was volunteering at the Red Cross emergency shelter at the convention center.

He sat at the information desk directing people where to go for help. All his possessions — his wallet and a bottle of soda — were at his side.

"A lot of people are a lot worse off than me. Think of the people who died, who lost loved ones. Why should I sit around and lick my wounds when I can help other people?"

— *Maria Goodavage*

The vacationers

Steve and Pam Slough had left Concord, N.C., for a week's vacation and a chance to escape the devastation left by Hurricane Hugo.

Slough, Concord's public utilities director, had spent two weeks working overtime and on weekends to restore power to the hurricane-ravaged city.

So he and his wife decided to use their free time during a water pollution conference in San Francisco to sightsee.

And that's what they were doing at Fisherman's Wharf when the earthquake struck. With cable car service knocked out, they walked two miles back to their hotel through debris.

"They're frightened — and so are we," Steve Slough's mother, Pearl, said. "I guess this trip didn't turn out the way they had planned."

All day Wednesday, the couple's friends and co-workers called relatives for the latest news. The Sloughs' two children stayed glued to the TV listening for news of the quake.

But family members had only had two brief conversations with the couple since Tuesday, and know very little.

"All they said is they're ready to come home," said Pam Slough's mother, Rachel Smith. "My prayers have been answered. She's the only child we've got and she doesn't react good to these kinds of situations."

— *Jack Kelley*

The driver

Bruce Stephan was sure he was going to die. The 33-year-old engineer was driving home with a co-worker on the upper deck of the Bay Bridge.

First, his car began to jump up and down. Then the portion of the bridge he was driving on collapsed. The car plunged from the upper deck onto the lower deck and nearly into San Francisco Bay.

"We were falling through the bridge and there was nothing to catch us," he said.

"Janice, we are going to die," he yelled to his passenger.

Suddenly a piece of the gnarled bridge caught the car and the pair dangled precariously above the water. "I saw water below us. I felt for sure we were going into the bay."

But the car stopped.

Stephan climbed out a window and dragged his dazed and bleeding companion to safety. Once outside the car, the pair walked to Treasure Island and "didn't look back."

"This is my second life," Stephan said after being released with minor injuries from San Francisco General Hospital Wednesday, "because I died back there."

— *Andrea Stone*

The golfer

Hugh Hunt, a visitor from Blair, Neb., was on the 18th fairway of Lincoln Park Golf Course.

"I was riding in a cart, and when it started I thought we had a couple flat tires," he said. "Then things really started happening, and we knew what it was. The trees started waving frantically. We were standing there and we could hear 'crack, crack, crack' from the trees breaking.

"It was kind of like taking a stick under a rug and moving it along. It didn't shake the whole area at once. It just moved through." And then, Hunt and his golfing partners finished their round.

"When it was over, we just finished. I hit the best shot I ever hit," he said. "I'm a terrible golfer, but I played one of my better holes."

Pacific Garden Mall, Santa Cruz

Community Development in a Seismically Active Region

You have witnessed the savage power of a major earthquake. In 1989, deep below a mountain in northern California, one of the earth's tectonic plates moved about six feet down the block, and will likely never move back.

In the 15 seconds that the Loma Prieta earthquake shook the earth, people in Santa Cruz and around the San Francisco Bay Area shared an experience that would change their lives for years—in some cases forever. There were people who lost their homes, their place of work, their schools, virtually their whole communities—and some lost their lives.

Our Earth has no regard for the effort we put into our creations. Even though it takes many skilled people years, even decades, to design and build magnificent skyscrapers, an earthquake—within a fraction of a minute—is capable of reducing a poorly-designed building to rubble. In many cases, the people responsible for the quality of the planning and construction for a building make the difference in whether a family is out on the streets and homeless, or still has a house or apartment in which they can safely live.

When people are away from human-made structures, they are usually not hurt by an earthquake. What is a city planner's responsibility for protecting the public in a disaster?

I was home after school doing my homework when the lights went off and the shaking occurred. We all ran outside.

Following the earthquake, I couldn't sleep very easily, and I didn't get a lot of food.

AYA YOSHIDA
CASTROVILLE, CALIFORNIA

Being an Expert

When experts such as architects, engineers, geologists, or city planners are working on a project, it is not so different from when you are doing your homework. Sometimes with a deadline pressing on them, they will spend long hours working at home also. Except, however, there is no teacher to check their work and no second chance to do it over after it fails. It must be done correctly the first time.

How do people earn the title of "expert"? They do their homework! With every decision they face, they make sure they have thoroughly researched the topic. They examine the work of other experts in their field, ask questions, and conduct experiments to test new theories if necessary.

Experts are also on the lookout for new ideas in areas outside their fields that could have relevance to their work. In 1991, a group called Habitat for Humanity built houses in southern Florida's hurricane territory. The dwellings were all constructed using a new process involving prefabricated polystyrene-and-wire panels sprayed with concrete. All fifteen Habitat houses located in the area survived the wrath of 1992's Hurricane Andrew, while frame-type houses in the area were destroyed. Would these Habitat houses survive a major earthquake?

Ethics

It is always a good policy to try to get as much funding for a project as possible and to try to save as much money as possible during planning and construction while still meeting the customer's requirements. Some people, however, are unscrupulous.

Some experts believe that many families in southern Florida lost their frame houses in Hurricane Andrew because of shoddy workmanship or shortcuts by companies that built houses during the building boom of the 1980s. The same is true in some cases of houses that have been destroyed in earthquakes.

Architects and engineers are looking at all aspects of the construction project. Where can they save money, but still be within the building code regulations? Maybe there is a new high-tech material, such as a composite material, that is strong but cheap.

While you are involved in the various earthquake-related activities and experiments in this project, try to develop new ideas and theories that could be tested by additional experiments.

Though there are many experts in earthquake science and master builders who understand stress and structures, there are still many unanswered questions concerning the survival of cities hit by earthquakes. You or your team of experts could, through your own experimentation and analysis, come up with answers that could save lives.

The Charge

You and your colleagues (classmates) will be working as experts to design a city. Five separate site-development teams will each select a different area of the world as the site for a planned city. The land on which each city is to be built must be in an area with a high risk of earthquakes. (When your team chooses its site, make sure it is in a country about which you can easily find information.)

Each site-development team will be composed of the following six experts:

Geologist
Chief of Transportation
Director of Utilities
City Planner
Architect
Civil Engineer

Choosing Your Expert Role

You and your site-development team members will each submit a prioritized list to your teacher with your role preferences (first choice, second choice, and so on). First choices will be assigned if possible.

Working Together

After selecting a general location, your team should use a world atlas to investigate the area. The requirements for the site are that it must

- Be within a square that is three miles wide on each side

- Include a body of water on one side

- Have existing highway access

- Have a varied terrain (hills, valleys, and so on)

Each team should develop a list of questions that they wish to have answered before they are ready to start. Activities that appear later in *Earthquake!* will provide background information and answer most of your questions.

As you work with your team, you should hold frequent expert-group sessions (meetings with other students in your class who have the same title as you) and less frequent whole-team working sessions. Communication is critical within teams and within expert groups.

As you work through the various aspects of this project, sharing information and developing new ideas, you should prepare materials that will be used in your final presentation. Materials created for the final presentation might include charts, tables, graphs, maps, taped or transcribed personal interviews, models, photos, or videotapes.

House east of Santa Cruz

Expert Tasks

Geologist: Conduct a geological study of the site of your community:

1. Draw a map of the actual site where the community will be built.

2. Locate a fault that runs through the site.

3. Identify where ground is likely to fail due to faults, liquefaction, or landslides.

4. Give a brief history of damaging earthquakes that have occurred in the region.

5. Estimate the probability of a damaging earthquake occurring in the region.

6. Identify areas that are suitable for housing (single-family houses, townhouses, apartments), industry, and commercial activities.

Chief of Transportation: Design a total transportation system for the community:

1. Draw a map or maps showing the location of each component of the transportation system. (The transportation system may include highways, bridges, railroad lines, airports, ports, marinas, and subways.)

2. Explain, in writing, special features that help adapt the transportation system to an earthquake zone.

3. Prepare plans explaining how the components of the system will work together to assist in providing emergency care and an orderly evacuation if necessary.

4. Consult with other experts so transportation facilities are located where they can best serve the community.

Director of Utilities: Plan the location of utility facilities (power plants, sewage treatment sites, water reservoirs, and pumping stations) and the distribution systems (pipelines, above-ground and underground wires, and so on):

1. Draw a map or maps showing the location of all community utility services (including water, electricity, sewer, gas, and so on).

2. Explain, in writing, special features that help adapt utility services to an earthquake zone.

3. Prepare an emergency-response plan that will help restore services and control losses due to interruptions following an earthquake.

4. Prioritize institutions that will need services restored immediately, and give reasons for the selected ranking.

5. Consult with other experts so utilities are located where they can best serve the community.

City Planner: Select the sites for all community facilities such as housing, shopping, industry, business, schools, hospitals, recreation facilities, fire and rescue stations, and police stations:

1. Consult with other experts on your team so community facilities are located where they can best serve the people.

2. Explain, in writing, features that help adapt the community to an earthquake zone.

3. Develop an emergency-response plan that will coordinate the efforts and resources of the agencies charged with public safety and assistance (police, fire department, hospitals, and so on).

4. Create a set of guidelines that can be used for damage assessment and emergency response.

Architect: Design buildings and assemble a three-dimensional model of the city plan:

1. Include one fault.

2. Include a body of water.

3. Include hills and valleys.

4. Include highways, bridges, railroad lines, airports, and so on as identified by the chief of transportation.

5. Include utility facilities as identified by the director of utilities.

6. Include buildings and other structures placed in the areas identified as safest by the team geologist.

Civil Engineer: Investigate design features necessary for the safest possible construction of roads, bridges, and buildings:

1. Consult with other experts so they are aware of your findings.

2. Design and build a model bridge that is earthquake resistant.

3. Assist the architect in constructing the city model.

4. Create a checklist of features that can be used to evaluate how earthquake resistant a house is. (Use the list to evaluate your own home and prepare a written report of suggested improvements.)

You and your team have the unique opportunity to benefit from the successes and failures of other city planners, architects, and engineers. By researching the construction methods and building materials—as well as the geology of the building site—used in other communities that have experienced an earthquake or other related disaster, your team can determine how to create a community that can withstand a large earthquake.

The Earth Quakes Every Thirty Seconds

More than one million earthquakes occur on our planet Earth each year. That is an average of one every 30 seconds, but many of these are too small to be felt and most occur in unpopulated areas around the rim of the Pacific Ocean. Nearly half the quakes that will rattle across the United States this year will take place in southern California.

The Loma Prieta earthquake of October, 1989, was the strongest quake to hit the San Francisco Bay Area since the great San Francisco earthquake on April 18, 1906. The 1906 disaster—estimated to have peaked at a magnitude 8.3 on the Richter scale—caused intense fires that swept through the city, covering 4 square miles, destroying more than 28,000 buildings, and taking the lives of about 700 people.

The Loma Prieta earthquake measured 7.1 on the Richter scale and was felt 800 miles away in Los Angeles. Thousands of aftershocks, measuring less in magnitude than the initial quake, continued to terrify already nervous residents.

Both the 1906 and 1989 earthquakes occurred along the infamous San Andreas fault. The San Andreas is the central fault. Fingers of other faults extend from the San Andreas, comprising a network of deep cracks covering more than 800 miles of California coastal region and snaking down to depths of at least 10 miles within the earth.

The San Andreas fault system stretches southward from northern California to Cajon Pass near San Bernardino. Southeastward from Cajon Pass, several branching faults, such as the San Jacinto and Banning faults, share the movement of two crustal plates.

STUDENT VOICES

After the quake, I didn't get much sleep. I was scared. Not many people went to school.

ERIC STARR
WATSONVILLE, CALIFORNIA

Perhaps you have heard the term "being rubbed the wrong way." In the language of an earthquake, it was the horizontal and vertical rubbing of the Pacific Plate and the North American Plate that created the Loma Prieta event. Movement occurred along a 25-mile segment of the San Andreas fault from southwest of Los Gatos to north of San Juan Bautista. In fact, the two plates normally move about two inches per year—in opposite directions. As these plates moved in relation to each other, the strain at their boundaries grew. When the pressure was too great, slippage occurred and the plates dramatically moved into a new position. That slippage generated vibration waves that we called an earthquake.

The Loma Prieta earthquake's epicenter—the point on the earth's surface directly above the earthquake's first movement—was in the Santa Cruz Mountains. From that epicenter, seismic waves radiated outward, in much the same manner as waves ripple out in all directions after you throw a rock into a still lake.

While seismic waves lose much of their energy as they travel over great distances, the Loma Prieta seismic waves destroyed many things as they rumbled along their destructive paths before they dampened out. Left in their wake were landslides and cracked ground, as well as fractured and buckled sidewalks, curbs, and streets. The price tag to rebuild state and local roads was estimated to be about $1.5 billion.

The area surrounding the Santa Cruz Mountains suffered the worst ground shaking, resulting in the damage or destruction of 30 percent of the structures located there. Many homes collapsed in the

Santa Cruz Mountains. Hardest hit in this region was the Pacific Garden Shopping Mall in downtown Santa Cruz. The violent shaking demolished or partially damaged 130 other buildings, many of which were designated 'historic' because they had been constructed in the nineteenth century. In this area alone, damage estimates were placed at $350 million.

Other locales 10 miles to 20 miles away from the quake's epicenter, such as Boulder Creek, Redwood Estates, Los Gatos, Scotts Valley, and Watsonville, each experienced intense ground shaking with significant damage to structures. About 30 miles northwest of the epicenter, at the Stanford University campus, 60 buildings were damaged—at an estimated repair cost of $160 million.

The Loma Prieta earthquake tallied more than $7 billion in property damage, with $2.5 billion of that figure in San Francisco destruction alone.

An earthquake's destructiveness depends on many factors. In fact, the magnitude of an earthquake does not necessarily cause the most intense effects above ground. In large measure, surface and subsurface geologic conditions of affected areas can be the real culprits.

For instance, buildings centered on unstable ground—such as land made up of underground layers of very wet soil, particularly sand—are usually more affected than similar structures situated atop ground composed of granite. Ground failure under this condition is called *liquefaction.* When shaken, sandy soils can be transformed from their solid state to a liquid, quicksand-like state.

In the Loma Prieta earthquake, liquefaction was the cause of major damage in San Francisco's

No area safe from quakes

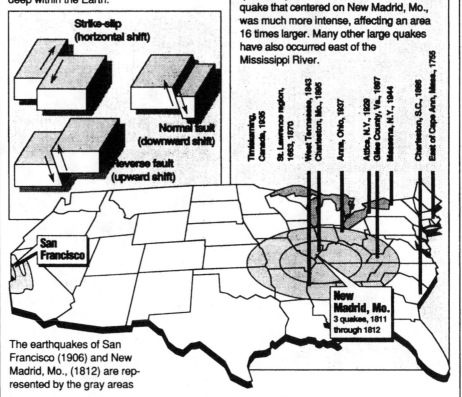

How they occur
Shifts along fault lines usually follow three basic patterns as a result of movements deep within the Earth.

Strike-slip (horizontal shift)

Normal fault (downward shift)

Reverse fault (upward shift)

Just as shaky back east
Though the 1906 San Francisco earthquake may be the best known, the 1812 quake that centered on New Madrid, Mo., was much more intense, affecting an area 16 times larger. Many other large quakes have also occurred east of the Mississippi River.

Timiskaming, Canada, 1935
St. Lawrence region, 1663, 1870
West Tennessee, 1843
Charleston, Mo., 1895
Anna, Ohio, 1937
Attica, N.Y., 1929
Giles County, Va., 1897
Massena, N.Y., 1944
Charleston, S.C., 1886
East of Cape Ann, Mass., 1755

San Francisco

New Madrid, Mo.
3 quakes, 1811 through 1812

The earthquakes of San Francisco (1906) and New Madrid, Mo., (1812) are represented by the gray areas

Source: USA TODAY research

By Keith Carter, USA TODAY

Marina District. The reason for such destruction is rooted in history as well as geology.

In 1906, the Marina District was a lagoon. Following the great earthquake that year, the lagoon became a dumping ground for sand and rubble from destroyed buildings. This filled land was used to create a fairground for the 1915 Panama-Pacific International Exposition. After the exposition closed, the land was transformed into a fashionable real-estate development called the Marina District.

When the rapidly traveling seismic waves from the Loma Prieta earthquake reached the silty layers of soil saturated with water in the Marina District, liquefaction took place. In addition, the deep, soft clay soils amplified the shaking. The liquefied soil and this amplification caused deformation of the ground. Its surface strength gone, the weakened

➤ continued on page 12

Marine Lab at San Jose State University

➤ continued from page 11

ground could not support many of the Marina District's buildings.

Along with liquefaction and amplified shaking, the way many of the buildings were designed—specifically the four-story buildings built above garages—greatly boosted the number of damaged structures in the Marina District. Many of these buildings had to be demolished because their inadequate lateral bracing made them structurally unsafe.

Liquefaction played havoc with buried underground utilities, such as water and gas pipelines, as well as sewer lines. These were heavily damaged, leaving about 1,000 homes in the Marina District without gas or water. Failed water mains prevented personnel from fighting the outbreak of fires in the Marina District—a situation similar to that of the 1906 earthquake. Water had to be pumped from a fireboat to extinguish many of the blazes.

As measured using the *Mercalli intensity scale*—a system in which quake damage is visually rated by trained observers on a scale ranging from I (very minor damage) to to XII (very great destruction)—the Marina District was rated from X to XI. Other parts of San Francisco, with buildings that rested on foundations other than loose soil, measured only VI or VII.

As cleanup operations began in the Marina District following the quake, crews noticed odd pieces of redwood and other materials brought to the surface by the liquefaction process. These curious fragments were from the 1906 quake, dumped there decades earlier as landfill. ∎

STUDENT VOICES

I was in my bedroom. The floor was shaking, and the drawers were opening and closing.

STEVEN GALVAN
WATSONVILLE, CALIFORNIA

The Structure of the Earth

Though we are rarely aware of it, the earth has a dynamic life of its own—one that brings changes on its surface and far below. To understand those changes, let's first consider the structure of our planet. The part we are most familiar with is the earth's crust. Like the skin of an avocado, it is very thin compared to the rest of the earth. This rocky crust measures between 3 miles and 12 miles thick under the oceans, and about 20 miles to 40 miles thick under land masses.

Under the earth's crust lies a layer called the *mantle*. Like the eatable part of an avocado, the

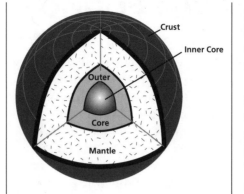

mantle makes up the bulk of the earth's volume. In fact, it reaches down some 1,800 miles, all the way to the core—which could be compared to the avocado's pit. Here, in the outer core, extremely high temperatures have melted the iron found

there to a molten liquid. The inner core is very hot but solid, compressed by the weight of the entire earth.

The study of earthquakes requires an understanding of the nature of the continental plates. The plates are different from the material beneath them. The plates, which consist of both crust and mantle, are rigid and the substructure is softer and more pliable, perhaps like soft clay, but no one is sure. One thing we are sure of: the mantle beneath the rigid plates moves, and upon it, the plates slip and slide—sometimes causing havoc for us on the surface.

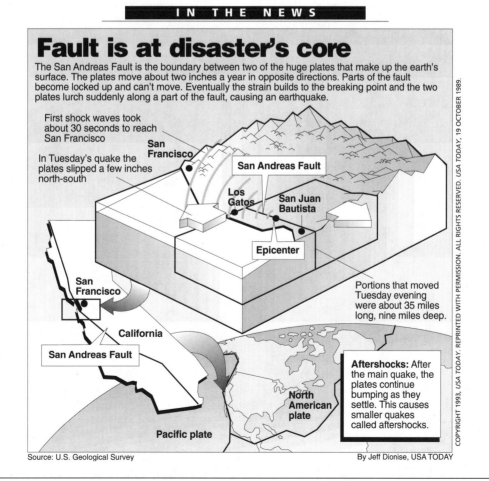

IN THE NEWS

Fault is at disaster's core

The San Andreas Fault is the boundary between two of the huge plates that make up the earth's surface. The plates move about two inches a year in opposite directions. Parts of the fault become locked up and can't move. Eventually the strain builds to the breaking point and the two plates lurch suddenly along a part of the fault, causing an earthquake.

First shock waves took about 30 seconds to reach San Francisco

In Tuesday's quake the plates slipped a few inches north-south

San Francisco

San Andreas Fault

Los Gatos

San Juan Bautista

Epicenter

Portions that moved Tuesday evening were about 35 miles long, nine miles deep.

San Francisco

California

San Andreas Fault

Aftershocks: After the main quake, the plates continue bumping as they settle. This causes smaller quakes called aftershocks.

North American plate

Pacific plate

Source: U.S. Geological Survey

By Jeff Dionise, USA TODAY

Where in the World Are Earthquakes Found?

Purpose
To identify regions of the earth where earthquakes occur and select possible sites for a city planning project.

Materials
- World map, page 15
- Earthquake List, below
- Colored pencils

Activity
Background: You and your partners work for a land development company specializing in building in earthquake territory. Your task requires you to select a site for a new city. The main requirement is that the site must be in a region of the world, besides California, where earthquakes regularly occur. You decide to use the Earthquake List below and a map of the world to construct an earthquake map. You should use that map to select and color four states or countries you think would make good sites for your team's city project.

As your group selects a country or state as a possible site for your city, remember that the city must:
- Be within a square three miles on each side
- Include a body of water on one side
- Have existing highway access
- Have hills and valleys

Do not forget to make a key and title your map.

Earthquake List					
Quake	Latitude	Longitude	Quake	Latitude	Longitude
1	50° N	170° W	26	0°	30° W
2	55° N	160° W	27	0°	20° W
3	60° N	154° W	28	0°	13° W
4	60° N	142° W	29	20° S	13° W
5	50° N	130° W	30	20° N	157° W
6	44° N	125° W	31	40° N	20° E
7	40° N	124° W	32	40° N	30° E
8	38° N	122° W	33	37° N	20° E
9	35° N	120° W	34	40° N	25° E
10	33° N	118° W	35	36° N	70° E
11	15° N	90° W	36	30° N	80° E
12	18° N	95° W	37	20° N	95° E
13	10° N	87° W	38	10° N	95° E
14	10° S	80° W	39	0°	100° E
15	20° S	70° W	40	10° S	110° E
16	30° S	70° W	41	50° N	180°
17	40° S	75° W	42	54° N	160° E
18	65° N	20° W	43	45° N	150° E
19	60° N	30° W	44	40° N	140° E
20	50° N	30° W	45	38° N	142° E
21	40° N	30° W	46	35° N	135° E
22	33° N	40° W	47	20° N	120° E
23	20° N	45° W	48	22° N	125° E
24	10° N	44° W	49	10° N	125° E
25	33° N	80° W	50	0°	123° E

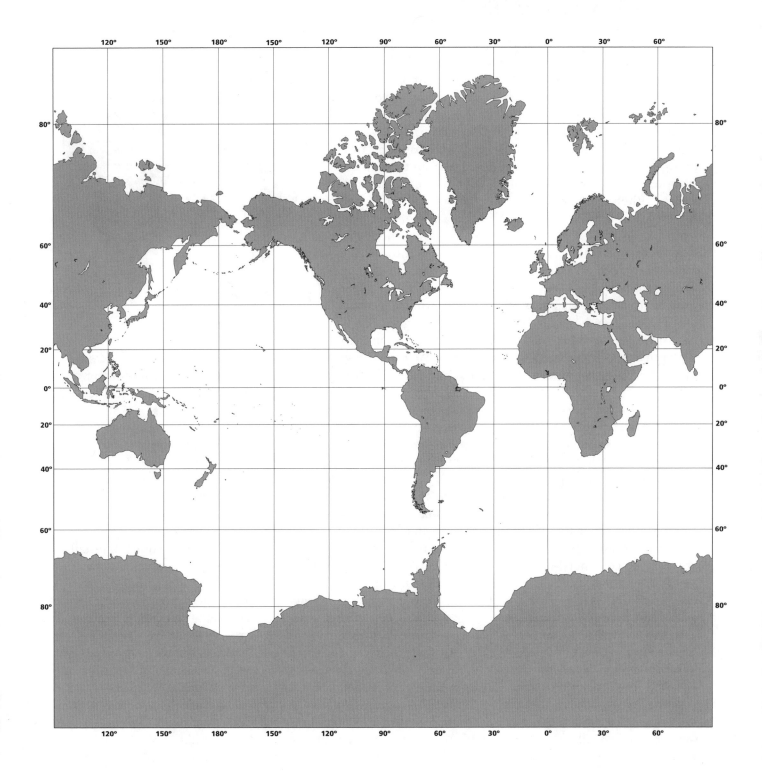

Tectonic Plates

Ever since the advent of world maps in the sixteenth century, people have remarked on the curious way in which the eastern coast of South America mirrors the western coast of Africa. It was not until the nineteenth century, though, that scientists discovered other parallel aspects. Botanists and naturalists exploring South America and Africa returned with some astonishing findings: There are striking similarities between the rocks of Brazil and the rocks of the Congo. Even more surprising, they found fossil remains of identical species of turtles, snakes, and lizards on both continents.

German meteorologist Alfred Wegener (1880–1930) finally gave scientific formulation to what people had been speculating for years. Somehow, the continents had once been joined together in one giant land mass that broke up into the continents we know today. Wegener was convinced that the world's continents, far from being fixed in one place, had drifted and were still drifting upon the surface of the earth.

Wegener's concept of *continental drift* met with ridicule in the 1920s, but further research continued to support his ideas. Scientists found evidence that over the past few million years, extreme climatic changes have occurred in certain parts of the world. The tropics, for instance, were once centered in areas now at the poles, and Africa was once covered with ice. These climate changes mark one way we know that land masses have drifted around the face of the globe.

Additional proof came from the dating of mid-ocean ridges at the bottom of the oceans. Scientists discovered that the rocks at the top of the underwater ridges were younger than rocks farther down slope, and much younger still than the rocks on continents. We now know that mid-ocean ridges form where heat currents from the earth's mantle reach the ocean crusts. In a process known as *ocean spreading*, the pressure splits the ocean floor, and the molten rock gushes up from the mantle, then cools to form an additional part of the ridge. Along with ocean spreading comes a parallel phenomenon: Old ocean crust is swallowed up into the mantle and destroyed along the deep trenches at the edge of the ocean. This process is known as *subduction.*

Most scientists today accept the theory of *plate tectonics*— from the Greek *tektonicos* for "builder"— as an extension of continental drift. According to this theory, the earth's surface is made up of about ten large plates and a number of small ones that fit together like a jigsaw puzzle. Each plate is composed of the earth's crust

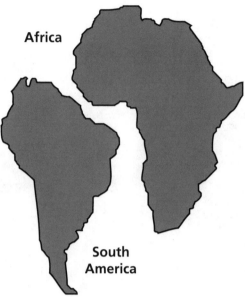

Africa

South America

and the top portion of the mantle, for a total thickness of about 100 miles.

Plates are constantly moving, though slowly. For example, the European and North American plates are estimated to be moving 7 centimeters (3 inches) farther apart each year. This is approximately the growth rate of your fingernails.

So mid-ocean ridges are spreading apart, and where plates meet, rock periodically accumulates strain. When the stress exceeds the strength of the rock, the rock ruptures—or breaks—along a pre-existing or new fracture plane known as a *fault.* When the rock ruptures, it causes the earth to tremble. This happens about 800,000 times a year. Usually faint tremors go unnoticed, but on occasion "the big one" for a region reminds us of the dynamic forces of our restless planet.

Faults

Earth's surface is always moving, and this movement causes cracks, called *faults*, in the crust. Faults often occur at the edges of tectonic plates, where one plate meets another or where the two portions of Earth's surface pull apart. However, faults can also appear anywhere the rocks in the crust have broken and no longer line up properly.

California's San Andreas fault, which was responsible for the 1906 San Francisco earthquake, is the best-known fault in the continental United States. Along this fault line, two large tectonic plates—the Pacific and the North American—come together. For hundreds of thousands of years, the Pacific Plate has been moving northwest at a rate of about 2 inches a year. As the plate moves, its edges sometimes "snag" the edges of the North American Plate. Since the remaining lower part of the plate continues to move along the softer upper mantle, stress builds up along the locked portion of the fault nearer the surface. This stress in the rock will eventually

Cypress Structure, Highway 880

become so great that it breaks, sending out shock waves in the form of an earthquake.

Faults give a distinctive character to the earth's landscape. We owe to faulting the Great Rift Valley, a giant trough that winds its way over thousands of miles from Turkey to Mozambique. Similarly, numerous mountain ranges throughout the world were caused by faulting (for example, the Himalayas, the Alps, and the Sierras).

Nature provides us with several different types of faulting. Vertical movement on a fault plane that is caused by extension is called *normal faulting*. Movement that is caused by compression is called *reverse faulting*. And faulting that appears to move in a sideways fashion is termed *strike-slip faulting*. Whatever the type, though, faults may lie dormant for decades, or even centuries, before the pressure exerted within makes them stir to life.

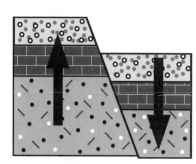

Normal Fault

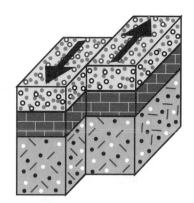

Strike-Slip Fault

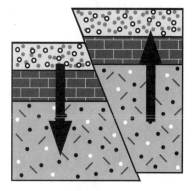

Reverse Fault

Civil Engineer

BOB MCBEAN
BLACK & VEATCH
ENGINEERS-ARCHITECTS
KANSAS CITY, MISSOURI

I am a civil engineer. Civil engineers design and manage the construction of power plants, water and sewage treatment plants, factories, office buildings, airports, roads, and bridges. I work in an office as do most engineers; occasionally I visit a construction site.

As a boy, I often helped my father, who was a maker of fine furniture, so it was natural that I had an interest in building things. In high school, I decided applied sciences, rather than pure sciences, most interested me. I also had an interest in art, so I was attracted to the aesthetic features of long bridges and high-rise buildings. In college, I really was turned on by the sophisticated computerized analysis we used to study failures of tall towers, buildings, and long-span bridges.

I like having a variety of technical assignments and working with people. I am continually challenged; rarely have I done the same type of work twice. I have developed a scheme for constructing a suspension bridge, designed the structure for a major office building, designed a 720-foot-tall chimney

for construction in India, and been involved in the structural design of several nuclear- and coal-fueled power plants. I have even traveled to Europe several times to meet with equipment suppliers. Most of what I have done has been exciting.

To become any kind of engineer, I recommend a teenager take a balanced but rigorous program in high school to prepare for the self-discipline needed at college and in the "outside world." He or she should take as much mathematics and physics as the school provides. Communication skills (writing and public speaking) are also very important to career development. Even typing skills are important in this computer age. Since most engineers are involved in the business world,

knowing the fundamentals of economics and finance is helpful. Finally, because United States companies must now compete for international work, I would recommend a course in world geography and a few semesters of a foreign language.

If you are the civil engineer on your city design team, ask your teacher to give you the FEMA booklet called the "Non-Technical Explanation of NEHRP Recommended Provisions" (available free from Building Seismic Safety Council; 1201 L Street NW, Suite 400; Washington, DC 20005). It should help you and your team's architect complete your parts of the task.

Measuring Earthquakes

How do we measure earthquakes and compare one to another? Scientists use an instrument called a *seismometer* or a *seismograph* to measure earthquake shocks. When the earth shakes, a freely suspended, heavy weight attached to a recording needle records the occurrence of the earthquake as a zigzag line on a paper-covered revolving drum or as digital data on a computer. The resulting graph is known as a *seismogram*.

A network of hundreds of seismograph stations all over the world work together to pinpoint the *focus* of an earthquake (the point within the earth's crust where the initial slipping of the faults actually took place) and the *epicenter* (the point on the earth's surface directly above the focus).

Scientists express the *magnitude* of an earthquake, which is proportional to the amount of energy released at the epicenter, as a figure on the Richter scale. This scale was named after the American seismologist Charles Richter, who designed it in 1935. The scale rates imperceptible tremors at the lower end and has no maximum, though any quake measuring 6.0 or more is considered major. The highest Richter magnitude ever recorded was 8.9 in the Pacific Ocean near the border between Columbia and Ecuador in 1906, and again in Japan in 1933.

An important aspect of earthquakes that most people do not realize is that above magnitude 6.7, the shaking does not get any stronger as the earthquake size increases (for observers within 100 miles of the epicenter). The shaking just lasts longer. A magnitude 7.0 event might cause the ground to move back and forth at a speed of 1 foot per second for about 15 seconds, whereas an 8.3 would cause the ground to move at the same speed but for about 45 seconds. The 1960 Chile earthquake lasted 4 minutes.

On the Richter scale, an increase of one whole number indicates a tenfold increase in ground motion and a 30-fold increase in radiated energy. A medium earthquake of 5.0, for example, would indicate a release of energy equal to the explosion of 10,000 tons of dynamite. A reading of 6.0 would correspond to the energy released by 300,000 tons of dynamite.

Whereas the Richter scale gauges the actual power of a quake, the modified Mercalli scale measures its effects on humans and buildings. It is based on a twelve-point scale ranging from I, with barely detectable vibrations, to XII, where damage is total and vibrations distort lines of sight and throw objects into the air. Observations of damage will vary according to the proximity to the epicenter and type of soil through which the shock waves travel.

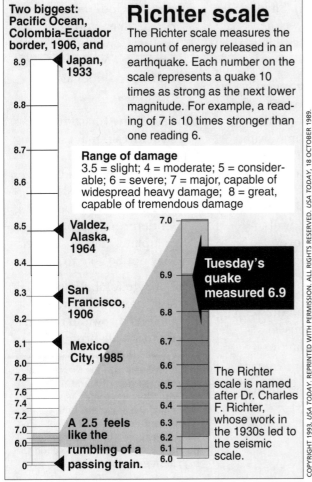

Two biggest: Pacific Ocean, Colombia-Ecuador border, 1906, and Japan, 1933

Richter scale

The Richter scale measures the amount of energy released in an earthquake. Each number on the scale represents a quake 10 times as strong as the next lower magnitude. For example, a reading of 7 is 10 times stronger than one reading 6.

Range of damage
3.5 = slight; 4 = moderate; 5 = considerable; 6 = severe; 7 = major, capable of widespread heavy damage; 8 = great, capable of tremendous damage

Valdez, Alaska, 1964

San Francisco, 1906

Mexico City, 1985

A 2.5 feels like the rumbling of a passing train.

Tuesday's quake measured 6.9

The Richter scale is named after Dr. Charles F. Richter, whose work in the 1930s led to the seismic scale.

Source: USA TODAY research   By John Sherlock, USA TODAY

Modified Mercalli Intensity Scale (Revised)

The following is an abbreviated description of the twelve levels of the modified Mercalli intensity scale.

I) Felt only by a few people under especially favorable conditions.

II) Felt only by a few people at rest, especially on the upper floors of buildings. Some hanging objects may swing.

III) Felt quite noticeably by people indoors, especially on the upper floors of buildings. Many people do not recognize that it is an earthquake. Standing cars may rock slightly. Vibration is similar to the passing of a truck.

IV) Felt indoors by many, outdoors by few; some sleeping people awakened. Dishes, windows, doors disturbed; walls make cracking sounds. Sensation like heavy truck striking building. Standing motor cars rocked noticeably.

V) Felt by nearly everyone; many sleeping people awakened. Some dishes and windows broken. Unstable object overturned. Pendulum clocks may stop. Swaying of tall trees and poles sometimes noticed.

VI) Felt by all; many people frightened. Some heavy furniture moved; a few instances of fallen plaster. Damage slight. Books fall off shelves and people walk unsteadily.

VII) Damage negligible in buildings of good design and construction; slight to moderate damage in well-built ordinary structures; considerable damage in poorly built or badly designed structures. Some chimneys broken. Small landslides and cave-ins along sand or gravel banks. Large bells ring.

VIII) Damage slight in specially designed structures; considerable in ordinary substantial buildings, with partial collapse. Damage great in poorly built structures. Fall of chimneys, factory stacks, columns, monuments, and walls. Heavy furniture overturned. Decayed pilings broken off. Branches broken from trees. Cracks in wet ground and on steep slopes. Frame houses moved on foundations if not bolted down.

IX) Damage considerable in specially designed structures; well-designed frame structures thrown out of plumb. Damage great in substantial buildings, with partial collapse. Buildings shifted off foundations. Serious damage to reservoirs. Underground pipes broken. Conspicuous cracks in ground; liquefaction.

X) Some well-built wooden structures destroyed; most masonry structures and frame structures with foundations destroyed. Rails bent. Serious damage to dams, dikes, and embankments. Considerable landslides on river banks and steep slopes along highways.

XI) Few, if any (masonry) structures remain standing. Bridges destroyed. Rails bent greatly. Broad fissures in ground; earth slumps and landslides widespread. Underground pipes completely out of service. May not be able to walk.

XII) Damage total. Lines of sight and level are distorted. Objects thrown in the air. Cannot walk or stand.

Note: A problem with the Mercalli scale is seen at intensities of X and XI. These two intensities are sometimes assigned when mild shaking reacts with water-logged sandy soil to cause liquefaction. This is one reason that high Mercalli numbers do not always correspond to high Richter numbers.

Waves

When an earthquake occurs, shock waves of energy flow out in all directions from the *hypocenter*—the underground point where the continental plates slide over or past each other releasing built-up stress. (Earthquakes can also occur along old faults in the middle of plates.)

Different types of waves work together to make up an earthquake. Primary, or *P*, waves exert a push-and-pull effect as they compress and expand the material they travel through, either liquids or solids. Since *P* waves travel through liquid, they can reach all the way to the core of the earth and out to the other side of the planet. *P* waves strike with hammer-like force, reaching a speed of 4 miles per second (15,000 miles per hour) in the crust of the earth and 8.5 miles per second in the core. They are often the first warning that a quake has happened.

Secondary, or *S*, waves are slower than *P* waves, traveling at little more than half their speed. *S* waves account for the up-and-down motion of the earth and the rippling of the ground common to earthquakes. Unlike *P* waves, *S* waves cannot pass through liquid and therefore do not pass through the earth's core.

P waves and *S* waves are known together as *body waves*. Scientists also speak of *surface waves*, the slowest of all waves. As their name suggests, surface waves travel along the surface of the earth. In the 1960 earthquake in Chile, surface waves were so powerful they were still being recorded on seismograms 60 hours after the event, having traveled around the earth 20 times. Most of the energy transmitted in shallow earthquakes comes in the form of surface waves, but it is the *S* waves that are used to determine the quake's magnitude on the Richter scale.

Earthquake Damage—Liquefaction

How do the seismic waves of an earthquake cause damage miles away from its epicenter? One major way is through the process of *liquefaction*. Imagine that the earth through which the waves pass is loosely compacted sediments, such as sand and silt. The stress of the quake may cause the groundwater to mix with these sediments as if in a great big blender, turning the whole zone to liquid. Liquefaction of the subsurface becomes one of the most damaging aspects of earthquakes occurring in populated areas. The land loses its weight-bearing capacity, and structures on the surface sink into the liquefied zone.

An example of severe damage caused by liquefaction can be found in the Turnagain Heights neighborhood of Anchorage, Alaska, during the 1964 earthquake. Turnagain Heights sits on a bluff overlooking Turnagain Arm, a bay off of Cook Inlet. Pockets of sandy soil several meters below the surface of Turnagain Heights liquefied during the quake. The overlaying soil slid around violently, causing the entire ground surface to slump toward Turnagain Arm, destroying most houses and other buildings in the neighborhood.

Liquefaction caused severe building damage in the 1906 San Francisco and 1989 Loma Prieta quakes as well, where the sandy fills underlying the Marina District of San Francisco lost their capacity to bear the weight of the structures built upon them.

We may also blame liquefaction for the landslides that often accompany earthquakes. When the slope is at a steep enough angle, and the underground granular layers are sufficiently saturated with water, large blocks of land can slide down the side of the slope, wreaking havoc as they comes to rest in the valley below.

Solid to Liquid in the Blink of an Eye: Liquefaction

What is *liquefaction*? According to standard dictionary definitions, it is simply the process of changing any substance into a liquid. In earthquake territory, this has special significance. When you mix loosely compacted sediments (usually sand and silts) with groundwater and shake well with an earthquake, potentially hazardous situations can occur.

The stress caused by the moving earth may rotate and move particles in groundwater-saturated zones. In motion, these saturated zones "liquefy." This process by itself is not a problem for people unless other conditions occur. If the unsaturated soil above the liquefied zone is either too thin or if it is unable to support large buildings when the subsurface zone liquefies, the surface soil loses its

bearing strength and sinks into the liquefied zone. This was the primary cause of building damage in the Marina District of San Francisco in the Loma Prieta earthquake of October 17, 1989, where liquefaction occurred in sandy landfills.

During liquefaction, the particles of sand or silt compact and increase the pressure in the pore spaces. This pressure pushes the particles apart, resulting in a

fluid mixture of sand and water that may be ejected to the surface to form sand boils. These explosive eruptions of sand and water mimic small volcanoes in both their activity and surface expression, often leaving behind crater-like features on the ground. In the Marina District, many areas experienced sand boils, a surface expression of the subsurface liquefaction process at work.

What about landslides? The hidden culprit in some landslide activity may be liquefaction. If the slope of the ground and the extent of the liquefied strata are favorable, large blocks of land can slide on these water-saturated loose granular layers. In the 1971 San Fernando earthquake, landslides due to liquefaction occurred within the lower San Fernando Dam at Van Norman Lake and nearly caused a major, uncontrolled release of the reservoir.

Liquefaction is proving to be one of the most damaging aspects of earthquakes. Scientific study of the liquefaction process and mapping of potentially hazardous areas are helping to reduce potential loss of property and life by providing input to sound engineering and construction.

SOURCE: US GEOLOGICAL SURVEY, US DEPARTMENT OF THE INTERIOR

House near epicenter

What Is Liquefaction?

Purpose

To investigate conditions that produce liquefaction during an earthquake.

Materials

- 2 large clear containers
- Tubing
- Water
- 2 rocks
- Sand
- Gravel

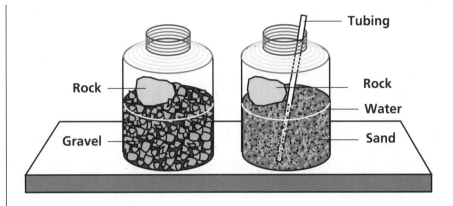

Activity

Background: You and your partners are experts on earthquakes. Your company just received a contract from the Alaskan state government to evaluate two possible building sites for a new state office building within Anchorage. Both sites are frequently shaken by earthquakes, but one site is located on sandy soil that is constantly saturated with water and the other site lies on bedrock. You and your partners decide to conduct an experiment before you write your recommendation.

1. Read Solid to Liquid in the Blink of an Eye, page 22.

2. Using the materials listed, construct a model of the two sites.

Note: When you add water to the sand, add it slowly and watch it fill the spaces between the grains. Keep adding water until it is just below the surface of the sand.

3. Wait a minute or two for everything to settle, then pound on the table with your fist to simulate an earthquake.

4. Pay particular attention to the rock. It represents a building or other heavy object on the surface.

Conclusions

Now prepare a brief memo for your supervisor in which you comment on the suitability of the two sites. Make your recommendation based on your understanding of liquefaction. State the reasons for your recommendation in words your supervisor will understand. (She is not a scientist.)

San Francisco Marina District

Heroes and Lessons

Despite the death and destruction caused by the Loma Prieta earthquake, good engineering and construction practices did decrease the number of lives lost and the amount of property destroyed. For several years, the San Francisco Bay Area had enforced new building codes designed to minimize a structure's vulnerability to earthquakes.

Examples of poorly constructed buildings—structures that could not withstand the Loma Prieta earthquake—were numerous, however: department stores sustained extensive damage due to weak first stories or insufficient reinforcement of stand-alone support columns, and older buildings were damaged due to deterioration of their primary structures or the use of unreinforced brick or stone masonry.

As with most earthquakes, the actual movement of the ground during the Loma Prieta quake was not likely to have directly caused the death or injury of any individual. Many casualties were the result of falling objects and debris stirred by the rumbling earthquake. Collapsing walls, toppling chimneys, falling brick from wall facings and roof parapets, overturned bookcases, fires from broken gas lines, and falling glass from shattered windows, particularly from high-rise structures, were identified as the real destructive villains in the Loma Prieta earthquake.

But these were not the only things set in motion by the Loma Prieta cataclysm.

Instant heroes were seen—volunteers tended fire hoses, comforted the injured, crawled through debris to rescue children, and became temporary traffic officers. Bound together by a common tragedy, victims of the Loma Prieta quake began to help each other by, quite literally, picking up the pieces of each other's lives.

An area known for its temblors, San Francisco is considered one of the most prepared cities in the world to counter the devastating impact of a quake. City planners, architects, fire marshals, building inspectors, engineers, and others have worked together for many years shaping comprehensive plans to thwart the havoc that results from earthquakes.

Valuable lessons learned from the Loma Prieta earthquake are now a part of California history. New, better-designed buildings, to replace those that fell victim to the 1989 natural disaster, are being added to the skylines of San Francisco and the surrounding, quake-torn cities.

Builders use metal straps or braces as strengthening parts for seismic resistance; they make building frames that can tolerate greater degrees of destructive earthquake energy; and they more often use layers of rubber and steel underneath buildings to isolate the effects of shaking ground from the main structure. These techniques and others are being added to make the region as earthquake resistant as possible. And for good reason.

STUDENT VOICES

Just as I rang the doorbell at a neighbor's house, the lady ran out yelling, "Get away from the house. It's an earthquake!" My friend and I ran out into the street away from everything. After the earthquake, we had to evacuate our house for one and a half weeks because our fireplace had fallen apart and our house slipped on its foundation.

MORGAN MEYERS
SALINAS, CALIFORNIA

These actions are necessary in preparation for the next big earthquake in the San Francisco Bay Area. By studying the frequency of earthquakes in the region, scientists have determined that a magnitude 7.0 earthquake closer to a more populated area than the Loma Prieta quake is mathematically likely before the year 2020.

Though success in predicting earthquakes is very limited, some seismologists have devoted their careers to searching for early warning signals.

Teams of scientists, engineers, and city managers worldwide are working collectively to learn more about the dynamic nature of earthquakes, the response of structures and local geology to earthquakes, and techniques and technologies to thwart the ever-restless planet we live on. ■

Buildings could be built to take more

By Tom Squitieri
USA TODAY

An earthquake much more powerful than the 1906 temblor that leveled San Francisco would be needed to inflict the same amount of damage to the Bay Area today, experts said.

Engineers can design buildings to withstand any earthquake ever recorded. After that, it's anybody's guess.

"The problem is scientists don't know what the maximum design load is," said John Woods, a structural engineer in Alexandria, Va.

Adds Dr. Richard Wright of the National Institute for Standards and Technology: "We can take one as big as the one in 1906 without collapse." That San Francisco quake was 8.3.

Architects and seismologists have used that rocker as the basis for developing minimum building standards to buttress against future earthquakes.

Some, however, are wary of stronger earthquakes.

"With each increase in magnitude you have more damage. A lot more buildings collapse," said Lisa Kantor, of the Memphis State earthquake center.

According to the Federal Emergency Management Agency, an earthquake with the intensity of that in 1906 would kill 11,000 Bay Area residents, cause 12,000 serious injuries and damage $25 billion worth of property.

Safe building for a quake

Here are some ways buildings are designed to withstand the forces of an earthquake:

REINFORCING BUILDINGS
Use of metal straps, braces, or other strengthening parts for seismic resistance.

MOVING FRAMES
Some taller buildings have ductile frames that move with the earth. The frame thus absorbs much of the destructive energy of the earthquake.

ISOLATORS
State-of-the-art building construction. Bearings separate the ground from the building so if the ground shakes, the building does not.

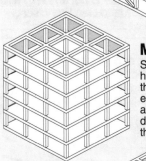

SHEAR WALLS
Installation of shear walls, which use reinforced concrete walls positioned perpendicular to each other, absorb the force that would otherwise crack the building.

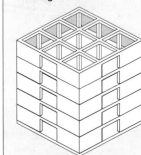

BUILDING SITE
Soft soil, such as a landfill, amplifies shock waves while rock tends to minimize the ground movement.

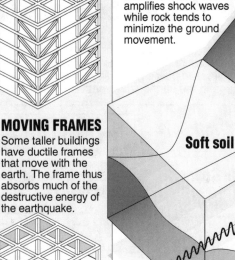

Soft soil

Rock

Seismic waves

UNDERGROUND BEARING
Cutaway view

Steel plate

Layers of rubber and steel

Steel plate

Source: Stanley Crawley, Professor of Architecture at University of Utah, author of *The Architect's Study Guide to Seismic and Lateral Loads*

By Juan Thomassie, USA TODAY

City Planner

DON ALSPACH
ANCHORAGE, ALASKA

A planner's job can be a very high-stress job. We are often presenting at meetings, serving on commissions, and working with community leaders. I spend most of my time answering questions on planning and zoning issues from the general public. I also interact with the utilities and public-works departments, as well as environmental agencies. If someone wants to get a new building approved, the request goes through my office. If someone is building a large structure in a central business district, under our zoning rules, we must do a "bonus-point calculation" to determine if the building will have sufficient amenities.

We have determined areas of Anchorage that have the highest susceptibility to ground failure. You should do that for your city, too. When someone proposes a project in one of those areas, we have them present their plans to our geo-technical commission. The geo-technical commission evaluates the project to make sure the risk is

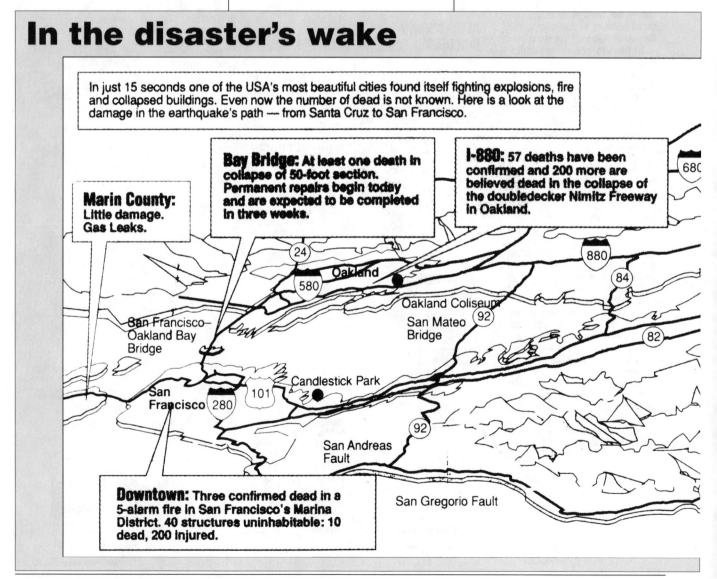

In the disaster's wake

In just 15 seconds one of the USA's most beautiful cities found itself fighting explosions, fire and collapsed buildings. Even now the number of dead is not known. Here is a look at the damage in the earthquake's path — from Santa Cruz to San Francisco.

Marin County: Little damage. Gas Leaks.

Bay Bridge: At least one death in collapse of 50-foot section. Permanent repairs begin today and are expected to be completed in three weeks.

I-880: 57 deaths have been confirmed and 200 more are believed dead in the collapse of the doubledecker Nimitz Freeway in Oakland.

Downtown: Three confirmed dead in a 5-alarm fire in San Francisco's Marina District. 40 structures uninhabitable: 10 dead, 200 injured.

San Francisco–Oakland Bay Bridge

Oakland Coliseum
San Mateo Bridge

Candlestick Park

San Francisco

San Andreas Fault

San Gregorio Fault

acceptable and the builder has taken into consideration the geological hazards present. They check whether the foundation has been modified to minimize the seismic risk. The geologists and engineers on that committee make their own evaluations. It usually ends up an engineer-to-engineer discussion.

The thing I like most about my job is seeing people come in with projects that have great promise, then watching the projects go through the process and actually be built. As a planner, I also like to see a developer who is sensitive to the natural surroundings and to the people around the project. It is fun to watch how a developer goes about negotiating with these people and resolving issues.

One of the best projects this department did was a coastal trail system. Along our coast, starting in the urban area, we have built a trail that runs along the edge of the water. It is an asphalt trail that is used by pedestrians, bicyclists, joggers, and roller skaters. You might consider such a feature for your city.

Planners have to do a lot of writing. Oral skills are important too, because planners speak to small groups as well as assembly meetings with several hundred people in the audience. A planner knows geography, geology, cartography (map making), and math. Planners calculate area and volume, slopes and building heights, density, floor-area ratios, percentages of lot coverage, and all sorts of other things. Skills with databases, spreadsheets, word processing, and typing are very important. It is also a good idea to have some knowledge of the environment (water quality, wetlands, air quality) and the law.

I got into this field after I took a course in cartography and was pretty good at it. This is a very good field for both men and women.

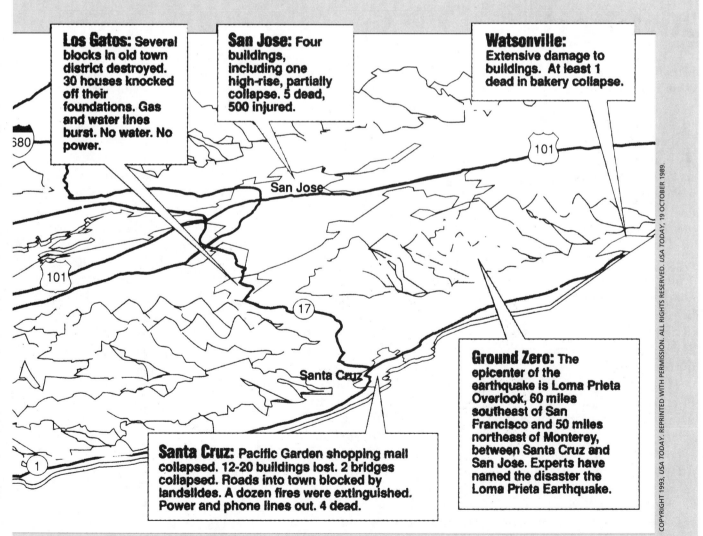

Los Gatos: Several blocks in old town district destroyed. 30 houses knocked off their foundations. Gas and water lines burst. No water. No power.

San Jose: Four buildings, including one high-rise, partially collapse. 5 dead, 500 injured.

Watsonville: Extensive damage to buildings. At least 1 dead in bakery collapse.

Ground Zero: The epicenter of the earthquake is Loma Prieta Overlook, 60 miles southeast of San Francisco and 50 miles northeast of Monterey, between Santa Cruz and San Jose. Experts have named the disaster the Loma Prieta Earthquake.

Santa Cruz: Pacific Garden shopping mall collapsed. 12-20 buildings lost. 2 bridges collapsed. Roads into town blocked by landslides. A dozen fires were extinguished. Power and phone lines out. 4 dead.

by Web Bryant and Julie Stacey, USA TODAY

Design Features

There are three design features that can be used to strengthen the framework of a building: brace, moment joint, and shear wall.

Brace: Wooden or metal beam attached diagonally to strengthen the frame of walls.

Moment Joint: A very strong connection between structural members that resists collapse.

(**Moment:** A force that causes bending in a building's frame.)

Shear Wall: Reinforced concrete walls positioned perpendicular to each other to absorb the force that would otherwise crack the building.

Architect

MICHAEL WANG
FAIRFAX, VIRGINIA

If you ask a builder to add a bedroom to your house, the builder will provide the space you want. An architect, however, will design a space that has deeper meaning, with more poetry than mere shelter.

I have always enjoyed drawing anything and everything. When I was growing up, I wanted to design my own house. So I became an architect. Now I design homes for other people. Maybe one day I will design one for myself.

On a typical day in the field, I check to make sure what is being built is in keeping with the intent of the drawings I made. I spend my time in the office drawing, coloring, and building models.

When we build our finer models, we usually use acid-free museum boards. We use chipboard for the regular models. Building models you see on display in museums are made out of Plexiglas® and cost between $50,000 and $300,000.

The thing I find most interesting about my work is the science of putting a building together from simple concept to reality. To an architect, every building is a minor miracle when it comes together well.

There are two directions in which to go if you are interested in architecture, design, or construction. You have to decide whether you want to get into the nuts and bolts of the architectural profession or the "pretty picture" side of things. Everybody thinks they want to get into the "pretty picture" part of it. But once they get into it, they realize that it is not all fun on that side. An ideal architect, one who can design *and* do production drawing *and* manage a project, needs to know a lot of math, geometry, physics, and history. History helps a lot. You cannot design things in a vacuum.

In California, part of the professional examination you must take deals with seismic design. But when it comes to the structural design of a building, liability is such a big issue in this country that, even if you know how, you would not want to touch it. Transfer the liability to the engineers. They are the real experts.

Earthquake-Resistant Building Designs

Purpose

To design a building that is earthquake resistant.

Materials

- 500 g mass
- 2 ring stands
- Steel rod
- Clamps
- 30 1" × 1" × 6" sticks of brittle plastic foam
- 10 wooden sticks
- 5 soda straws
- 8 ½" × 11" sheet of paper
- 8 ½" × 11" sheet of cardboard
- 3' length of string
- 20 thumbtacks
- 20 map tacks (longer pin than thumbtacks)
- 10 large paper clips
- 20 toothpicks (broken in half)
- Scissors
- Pennies or marbles
- 6"-diameter basket or similar container
- NO TAPE (tape defeats the purpose)

Activity

Background: Each month, a division of your company stages a friendly competition. These competitions require all employees to learn more about the work of the division that designs and sponsors the month's contest. Last month, the city planners challenged everyone to a SimCity® contest. This month the engineers have proposed an earthquake-resistant design competition.

Since you are probably unfamiliar with building design, the engineers suggest you read about the three design features they use to stiffen the framework of a building (braces, moment joints, and shear walls).

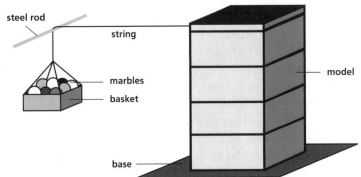

Contest Rules:

1. Using your imagination and the materials listed, construct a model of a building frame at least 18" high. Hint: Test your building as you go.
2. Mount your model within an 8" square on the cardboard. (Anchor the model to cardboard using a hot glue gun or strong glue.)
3. Test the vertical strength of the building by placing the 500 g mass on the roof. If the roof survives, go to the next step.
4. Test the lateral strength as shown above. (Carefully place pennies or marbles in the basket until the building fails.) This is the kind of force that is exerted on a building during an earthquake.

The winner is the group whose building supports the most pennies or marbles before it collapses.

Idea: Be sure to incorporate anything you learn about building design as you write building codes for your city.

House near epicenter

Earthquake Prediction

It was in the third century B.C. that the Chinese developed the first device known to detect and record earthquakes. A bronze vase with figures of serpents' heads near the top held small, bronze balls in their mouths. Whenever the slightest tremor occurred, the balls would fall into the open mouths of the frog figurines around the base of the vase.

But detecting and recording quakes is easy compared to predicting them. Many countries, including China, the former Soviet republics, Japan, Iceland, Italy, and the United States, are actively trying to predict earthquakes and are using equally ingenious ways to do so.

Scientists look for a change in the ability of crystal rock to conduct electricity, disturbance of the earth's magnetic field, or changes in the water level or temperature of deep wells in their attempt to pinpoint the next quake. Other devices pick up any shift within the earth. For example, the San Andreas Fault in California has been fitted with dozens of tiltmeters, which measure any tilt in a fault, as well as laser-ranging equipment sensitive enough to detect a change of a half inch in the earth's crust at a distance of five miles.

An intriguing aspect of earthquake prediction research is the theory that animal behavior can tip us off to an impending quake. Many Japanese claim goldfish begin to swim frantically just before a quake. Observers in China say that before an earthquake, snails come out of the ground, rats leave houses, birds refuse to roost, and dogs bark nonstop. It is possible that these animals sense something, and we just do not know what it is. As for goldfish, remember that water conducts sound waves and certain other waves better than some soils do.

As intriguing as these reports are, and in spite of studies of animals as diverse as cockroaches and chimpanzees, results so far have not been encouraging. Earthquake prediction remains an elusive goal.

IN THE NEWS

Calif. geyser can predict earthquakes

By Tim Friend
USA TODAY

A California geyser can forecast earthquakes up to 150 miles away, a report in today's journal *Science* shows.

But that finding is nothing new to Olga Kolbek, who's been recording eruptions by the Old Faithful Geyser of California on her property in Calistoga for 20 years.

"We've known the geyser correlated with earthquakes since Aug. 1, 1975," says Kolbek, who is "pushing 80."

"It erupts every 40 minutes on average, but for three days (before Aug. 1, 1975) it was erupting every 2½ hours. That night there was a quake 100 miles north of here that was 5.9 on the Richter scale."

The geyser, which is open to tourists, is 78 miles northwest of San Francisco on the northern edge of the San Andreas fault system.

After learning about Kolbek's records, geologists Paul Silver and Nathalle Valette-Silver, Carnegie Institution, Washington, D.C., correlated them and two years of their own monitoring with earthquakes over the past 20 years.

They concluded the geyser predicted at least three major California quakes, including the 7.1 Loma Prieta quake that rocked the San Francisco Bay area Oct. 17, 1989.

The researchers say the finding suggests other "old faithful-type geysers" may predict earthquakes as well.

One report shows the interval between eruptions at Old Faithful of Yellowstone slowed dramatically prior to a major earthquake there in 1959.

Kolbek says Old Faithful of California last predicted an earthquake Aug. 30.

"The interval had been building up in the last week, from 40 minutes to two hours again, and then we had a 4.2 on Sunday," Kolbek says.

USA TODAY, 4 OCTOBER 1992.

Earthquake Preparedness

When we think of earthquakes in this country, California springs to mind most often. Indeed, Californians have been waiting and planning for "the big one" for decades. But earthquakes can occur anywhere there is a fault line. In fact, the strongest earthquakes ever reported in the United States took place in the nineteenth century in Missouri.

What can you do to prepare for an earthquake? First, discuss earthquake preparedness within your family and run a practice drill: If shaking begins, protect yourself by ducking under a strong table or desk away from windows. Cover your head to protect yourself from debris or breaking glass. Never run outside during an earthquake. Just outside a building is the most dangerous place to be.

Develop an earthquake plan at home and at school. You may be separated from your family for several hours should an earthquake occur, so discuss within your family how you would handle such an emergency.

You can also store emergency supplies for use at the time of a disaster. Plan to include flashlights, a battery-operated radio, extra batteries, a fire extinguisher, a first-aid kit, food, water, water purification tablets, and warm clothes (including shoes) for everyone in the family. A scissors jack or hydraulic jack could save a life.

For cooking and heat, store charcoal or a camp stove with fuel, matches, and candles. Be sure to be very careful using the candles and other flammables, especially around young children.

Finally, if an earthquake does occur in your area, keep the following in mind:

- Do not panic. The shaking and rolling is frightening, but unless something falls on top of you, it is harmless. Keep calm and ride out the waves.
- If you are outside, stay away from buildings and utility wires.
- If you are in a car, stop and stay inside. A car is your safest place to be while the shaking continues.

Once the shaking stops remember to:

- Check your utilities. The movement may have cracked water mains, gas pipes, or electrical conduits. If you smell gas, open windows and shut off the main gas valve. Then leave the building and report the leak.
- Tune your radio to receive the latest emergency bulletins.
- Stay off the phone except to report emergencies.
- Stay out of severely damaged buildings. Aftershocks sometimes cause more damage than main shocks when they topple weakened buildings.

STUDENT VOICES

At the time of the earthquake, I was in the kitchen with my mom, dad, and three brothers. The plates, cups, and food were coming out of the shelves. I got my little brother and got under the dinner table. I told him that everything was okay because he was scared. During the first few days following the earthquake, I couldn't sleep because it might happen at night.

LAURA HUERTA
CASTROVILLE, CALIFORNIA

The Los Angeles Quake of 1994

In the early hours of Monday, January 17, 1994, residents of Los Angeles were violently awakened. A sudden darkness befell the hardest-hit areas as power lines snapped. Then, when the trembling stopped, blaring car alarms and the hiss of escaping natural gas pierced the quiet.

The quake that shook residents from their sleep was not as powerful as the Loma Prieta quake of 1989. But this, the Northridge earthquake of 1994, was equally destructive. It measured 6.6 on the Richter scale and caused death and destruction over a very wide area of Southern California. However, it was not the "big one" either.

This one was centered almost 10 miles beneath the San Fernando Valley on a previously unknown thrust fault. The fault ruptured for 6 seconds, and shaking was felt anywhere from 10 to 60 seconds. The violent movement lifted a huge piece of rock 1 foot to 3 feet, caused 57 deaths, injured more than 7,500 people, left about 15,000 homeless, and caused up to $30 billion in damages. It also left seismologists scrambling to explain what happened.

The famous Los Angeles freeways took a severe hit. The Santa Monica Freeway and other highways that serve as the arteries of this great city threatened to remain closed for up to a year, following the collapse of some elevated sections.

After a 1971 earthquake in the same area of Los Angeles, Caltrans (the California Transportation Department) began a program of strengthening bridges and overpasses in high-risk areas of the state. After the 1989 Loma Prieta quake, the strengthening program was expanded to include concrete columns supporting elevated highways in seismically active areas. Wrapping "jackets" around the columns helps them withstand shaking during an earthquake. Ironically, the Santa Monica Freeway was next on the list of roads to receive their earthquake-resistance treatment. Work was scheduled to begin only three weeks after the earthquake.

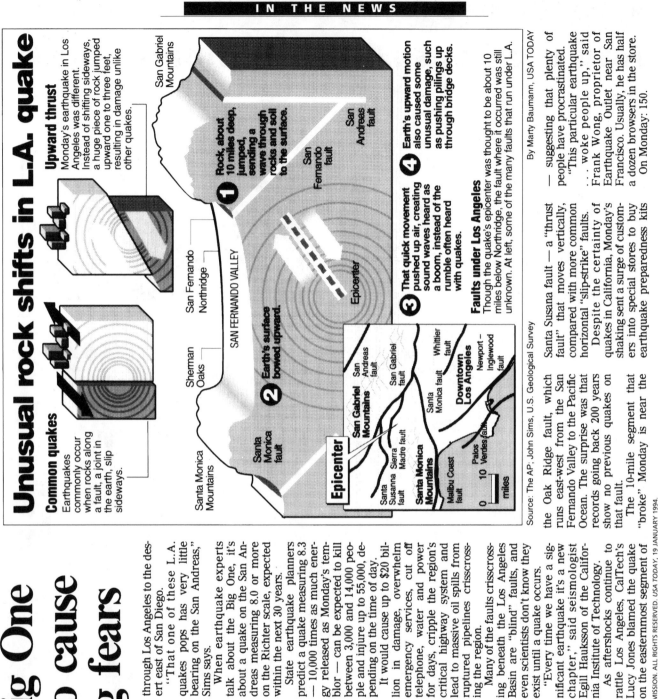

Unusual rock shifts in L.A. quake

Common quakes
Earthquakes commonly occur when rocks along a fault, a joint in the earth, slip sideways.

Upward thrust
Monday's earthquake in Los Angeles was different. Instead of shifting sideways, a huge piece of rock jumped upward one to three feet, resulting in damage unlike other quakes.

San Gabriel Mountains

Santa Monica Mountains

Sherman Oaks

San Fernando Northridge

SAN FERNANDO VALLEY

San Gabriel Mountains

San Fernando fault

San Andreas fault

1 Rock, about 10 miles deep, jumped, sending a wave through rocks and soil to the surface.

2 Earth's surface bowed upward.

Epicenter

3 That quick movement pushed up air, creating sound waves heard as a boom, instead of the rumble often heard with quakes.

4 Earth's upward motion also caused some unusual damage, such as pushing pilings up through bridge decks.

Epicenter

San Gabriel Mountains

San Andreas fault

San Gabriel fault

Whittier fault

Santa Monica fault

Downtown Los Angeles

Newport – Inglewood fault

Santa Susana fault

Sierra Madre fault

Santa Monica Mountains

Malibu Coast fault

Palos Verdes fault

0   10
miles

Faults under Los Angeles
Though the quake's epicenter was thought to be about 10 miles below Northridge, the fault where it occurred was still unknown. At left, some of the many faults that run under L.A.

Source: The AP; John Sims, U.S. Geological Survey

By Marty Baumann, USA TODAY

Pretty Big One enough to cause pretty big fears

By Maria Puente and Jack Williams
USA TODAY

The Big One — that monster earthquake every Californian dreads — is still to come.

But in the meantime, there's plenty to fear from the Pretty Big Ones, like the quake that startled Los Angeles Monday.

"There are tens of faults capable of producing 6.5 to 7.5 (Richter scale) quakes under the Los Angeles Basin," says John Sims of the U.S. Geological Survey.

On Tuesday, battered Los Angelenos awoke to some inescapably sobering facts — and a reminder that the real Big One inevitably will come:

▲ Monday's 6.6-magnitude quake occurred on a previously little-known fault — meaning not only another underground time bomb to worry about, but the likelihood of who-knows-how-many-others lurking unseen.

▲ Even a Pretty Big One can be catastrophic in a highly populated area: The toll from Monday is at least 40 dead, thousands homeless and perhaps billions of dollars in damage.

As bad as it was, Monday's quake did nothing to relieve the pressure on the San Andreas fault, the feared 650-mile gash running through the state's three largest urban areas, from San Francisco through Los Angeles to the desert east of San Diego.

"That one of these L.A. quakes pops has very little bearing on the San Andreas," Sims says.

When earthquake experts talk about the Big One, it's about a quake on the San Andreas measuring 8.0 or more on the Richter scale, expected within the next 30 years.

State earthquake planners predict a quake measuring 8.3 — 10,000 times as much energy released as Monday's temblor — can be expected to kill between 3,000 and 14,000 people and injure up to 55,000, depending on the time of day.

It would cause up to $20 billion in damage, overwhelm emergency services, cut off telephone, water and power for days, cripple the region's critical highway system and lead to massive oil spills from ruptured pipelines crisscrossing the region.

Many of the faults crisscrossing beneath the Los Angeles Basin are "blind" faults, and even scientists don't know they exist until a quake occurs.

"Every time we have a significant earthquake it's a new chapter," said seismologist Egill Hauksson of the California Institute of Technology.

As aftershocks continue to rattle Los Angeles, CalTech's Lucy Jones blamed the quake on the easternmost segment of the Oak Ridge fault, which runs east-west from the San Fernando Valley to the Pacific Ocean. The surprise was that records going back 200 years show no previous quakes on that fault.

The 10-mile segment that "broke" Monday is near the Santa Susana fault — a "thrust fault" that moves vertically, compared with more common horizontal "slip-strike" faults.

Despite the certainty of quakes in California, Monday's shaking sent a surge of customers into special stores to buy earthquake preparedness kits — suggesting that plenty of people have procrastinated.

"This particular earthquake . . . woke people up," said Frank Wong, proprietor of Earthquake Outlet near San Francisco. Usually, he has half a dozen browsers in the store. On Monday: 150.

And the House Came Tumbling Down

Purpose

To design an experiment that tests different methods for anchoring a house to resist landslides.

Materials

- Coarse sand
- Cardboard box at least 1' × 1' × 2'
- 4 large-diameter dowels about 1" × 1'
- Model house

Activity

Background: Landslides during the Loma Prieta earthquake caused damage costing tens of millions of dollars. The most common landslides were rock falls, rock slides, and soil slides. Landslides killed at least two people during that quake.

Your firm has just acquired land in a seismically active region of the world. There are hills on that land, and you have been asked if there is any way to build safely on the hillsides. Your team decides to divide into two- or three-person groups, each to test different design ideas. Tests are conducted in the sandbox by creating a sloping surface, mounting the model to be tested, and shaking the box vigorously to simulate the vibrations of an earthquake.

Following the tests, the team must write a recommendation in a memorandum to the president of your company. Be sure your recommendation makes sense from both an engineering and cost basis. Support your recommendation with data from your tests.

By Matt Mendelsohn, USA TODAY

HOMELESS: A home slides off a hilltop in Pacific Palisades. The 6.6 earthquake left at least 24,000 people homeless.

Geologist

CAROL PRENTICE
UNITED STATES
GEOLOGICAL SURVEY
MENLO PARK, CALIFORNIA

After a big earthquake, there are thousands of aftershocks that continue for years. Often there is what we call "after-slip." During an earthquake, there is a certain amount of slippage, then over the next day, week, or even months, the fault continues to slip. It is very interesting to measure to see how fast that happens. In some cases, it may be that little pulses of "after-slip" happened with aftershocks.

When an earthquake occurs and you look at the seismogram, you do not know whether or not a particular event is a pre-shock or a main-shock. You do not really know until something bigger happens or does not.

There are two things I love about my job. The first is that I have a lot of freedom and get to spend time outside. Second, I feel that what I do is very relevant to people's lives, and that is important to me.

The main thing I do is dig trenches across faults. I go as deep as I can, but not so deep that I put my life in jeopardy. A typical trench is between 10 feet and 15 feet deep. I study the face of the trench inch by inch.

In the state of California there is a law that if you are building *near* what has been designated by the state as an active fault zone, you have to have a geo-technical report. If you are building within the zone, a geologist has to come and dig a trench to make sure there are no active faults where you plan to place the building. If I were part of your site development team, I would insist on the same process for your planned city.

Math and physical science (physics and chemistry) are important to a geologist. History is helpful to a paleo-seismologist. Camping skills are also helpful.

When you are talking about the size of an earthquake, there are really two different ways of thinking about it. There is the *intensity* of an earthquake, which has to do with the amount of shaking and damage. There is also the *magnitude* of an earthquake. Magnitude has to do with the amount of energy released. When we study California earthquakes that occurred in the nineteenth century, there is really no instrumentation to tell us much about the energy released. We try to estimate the intensity based on damage reports from newspaper articles and people's journals and letters. An intensity reading gives us a general idea of what the magnitude was. We measure intensity on the Mercalli scale.

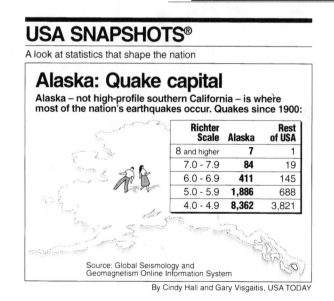

USA SNAPSHOTS®

A look at statistics that shape the nation

Alaska: Quake capital

Alaska – not high-profile southern California – is where most of the nation's earthquakes occur. Quakes since 1900:

Richter Scale	Alaska	Rest of USA
8 and higher	7	1
7.0 - 7.9	84	19
6.0 - 6.9	411	145
5.0 - 5.9	1,886	688
4.0 - 4.9	8,362	3,821

Source: Global Seismology and Geomagnetism Online Information System

By Cindy Hall and Gary Visgaitis, USA TODAY

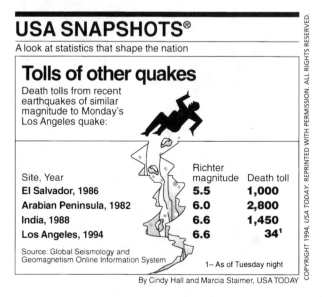

USA SNAPSHOTS®

A look at statistics that shape the nation

Tolls of other quakes

Death tolls from recent earthquakes of similar magnitude to Monday's Los Angeles quake:

Site, Year	Richter magnitude	Death toll
El Salvador, 1986	5.5	1,000
Arabian Peninsula, 1982	6.0	2,800
India, 1988	6.6	1,450
Los Angeles, 1994	6.6	34[1]

Source: Global Seismology and Geomagnetism Online Information System

1– As of Tuesday night

By Cindy Hall and Marcia Staimer, USA TODAY

A look at L.A. freeway overpasses

Experts are trying to determine exactly how several California freeways collapsed during Monday's earthquake. They are looking at whether steel restraining cables failed or concrete support columns crumbled, as well as whether unusually strong vertical forces caused a new type of failure. The Interstate 5 overpass:

Improving the expansion joints

ORIGINAL

RETROFITTED
Steel restraining cables added so spans won't move too far and topple.

NEW CONSTRUCTION
Increase overlap distance between new road spans.

Retrofitting

After the 1971 quake in Sylmar, California began retrofitting bridges and columns. Then, after the 1989 quake in northern California, the state began a more ambitious $1.5 billion program to retrofit 900 overpasses. About 300 are in progress or finished.

Road may have separated at expansion joint or at connection to support column.

Overpass deck is one piece of reinforced concrete.

Highway decks overlap at expansion joints.

Support column and deck are connected by steel rods inside concrete.

HIGHWAY 14

NEW CONSTRUCTION
Reinforcing steel is wrapped around rebars before concrete is poured.

INTERSTATE 5

Improving the columns

ORIGINAL
Concrete

Steel support bars called rebars

RETROFITTED
Steel ties added

Steel jackets — 1/2" to 3/4" thick — are welded around steel ties and existing columns to hold concrete in place.

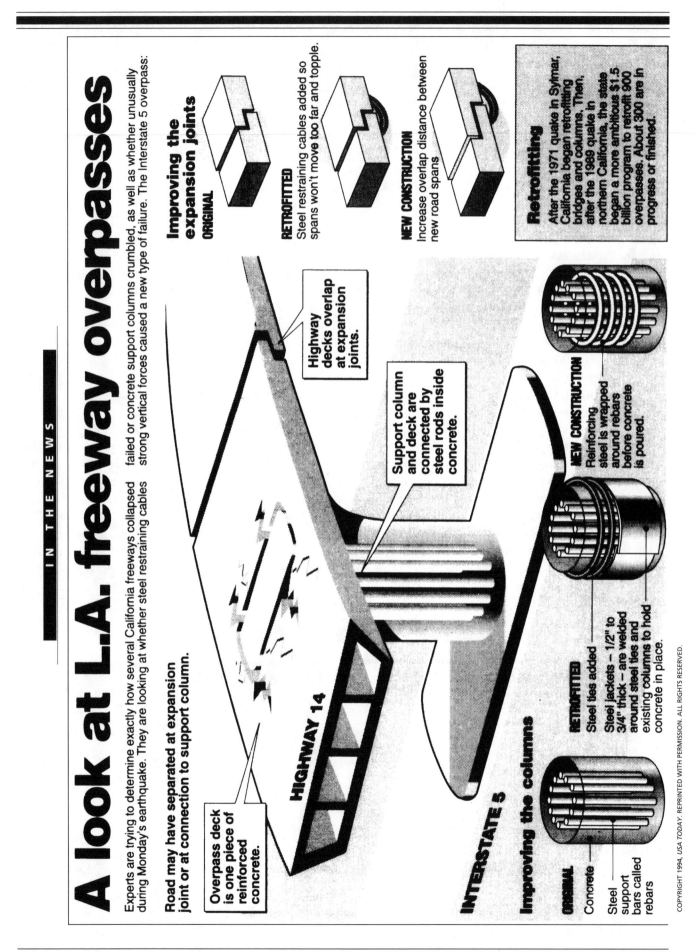

Closings put commuters on edge

Closings of parts of major freeways and highways across the Los Angeles Basin has commuters scrambling onto small roads and finding gridlock on city streets. And the California Department of Transportation says it could take a year to 18 months to fix the highways. The situation:

Love affair with cars

Before the quake, the average commute took Los Angeles area drivers about a half-hour. How they commute:

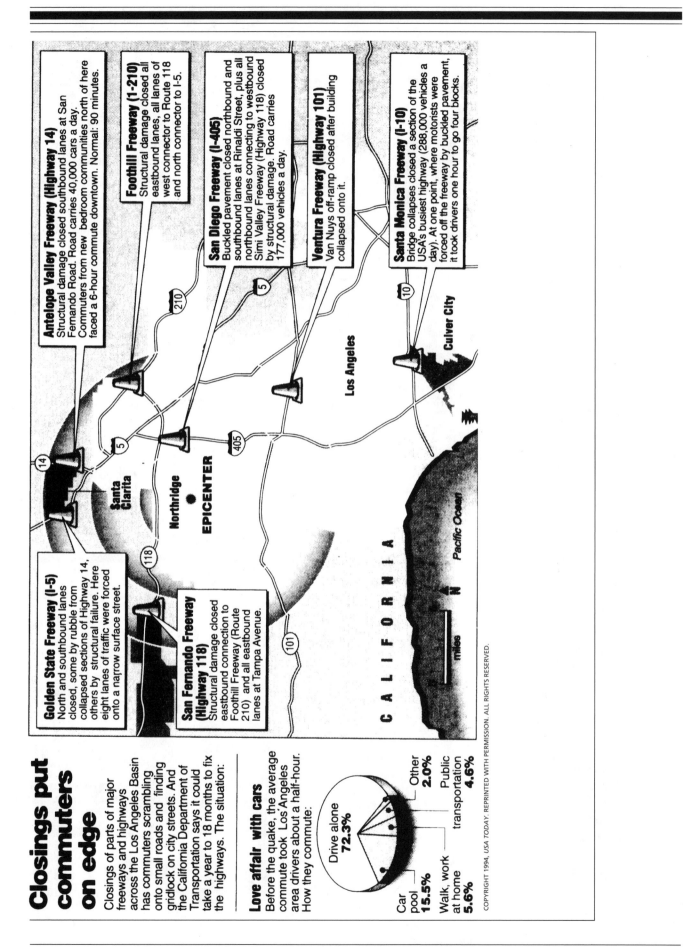

Car pool **15.5%**

Walk, work at home **5.6%**

Drive alone **72.3%**

Other **2.0%**

Public transportation **4.6%**

Golden State Freeway (I-5)
North and southbound lanes closed, some by rubble from collapsed sections of Highway 14, others by structural failure. Here eight lanes of traffic were forced onto a narrow surface street.

San Fernando Freeway (Highway 118)
Structural damage closed eastbound connection to Foothill Freeway (Route 210) and all eastbound lanes at Tampa Avenue.

Antelope Valley Freeway (Highway 14)
Structural damage closed southbound lanes at San Fernando Road. Road carries 40,000 cars a day. Commuters from new bedroom communities north of here faced a 6-hour commute downtown. Normal: 90 minutes.

Foothill Freeway (I-210)
Structural damage closed all eastbound lanes, all lanes of west connector to Route 118 and north connector to I-5.

San Diego Freeway (I-405)
Buckled pavement closed northbound and southbound lanes at Rinaldi Street, plus all northbound lanes connecting to westbound Simi Valley Freeway (Highway 118) closed by structural damage. Road carries 177,000 vehicles a day.

Ventura Freeway (Highway 101)
Van Nuys off-ramp closed after building collapsed onto it.

Santa Monica Freeway (I-10)
Bridge collapses closed a section of the USA's busiest highway (288,000 vehicles a day). At one point, where motorists were forced off the freeway by buckled pavement, it took drivers one hour to go four blocks.

Santa Clarita

Northridge

EPICENTER

Los Angeles

Culver City

CALIFORNIA

Pacific Ocean

N

miles

Chief of Transportation

James E. Roberts
California Department of
Transportation
Division of Structures
Sacramento, California

I got interested in transportation engineering and design because my dad was a building contractor. I stayed with it because engineering is a fascinating field; it is always changing.

After the San Fernando, California, earthquake of 1971, we changed our seismic design criteria considerably. Now, when we try to bring older bridges up to the current seismic standards, it causes serious traffic problems. In urban areas, we have right-of-way problems, and we are forced to do a lot of work at night and on weekends. We also run into underground utilities and other things that were not there thirty years ago when the bridges were built. Starting from scratch is much easier.

When we design a new bridge, we try to make the columns that support the bridge more flexibly. *Flexibility* means you can bend something back and forth without breaking it. If a bridge has a flexible support system, it will ride through many vibrations in an earthquake. You might get some minor damage that is easily repaired, but you will not get a collapse such as in the 1971 San Fernando earthquake or the 1989 Loma Prieta quake.

What I like most about my job is the fact that when I go home at night, I can talk about the things I've designed. I have pictures all over the walls of my office of bridges, a light-rail system, and other interesting projects I've worked on. I feel a great deal of satisfaction about my contribution to society.

To be successful in transportation, you have to have a bachelor's degree in civil engineering. The field is so technical there is too much to cover in a four-year curriculum; so, to get ahead, you need a master's degree. On-the-job experience is also critical. Get a strong background in math and physics. A lot of structural work and dynamics is really an extension of physics. Typing is helpful, because somewhere along the line you are going to be writing reports. In my everyday work, I use my knowledge of physics, math, and computer technology. My knowledge of geoscience is used for specialized projects.

When you plan your city, do not be afraid to include a subway. Underground, deep in bedrock, is a safe place to be during an earthquake.

IN THE NEWS

USA SNAPSHOTS®
A look at statistics that shape the nation

How often quakes occur

Richter scale magnitude	World-wide occurrence
8 and higher	1 per year
7.0-7.9	18 per year
6.0-6.9	120 per year
5.0-5.9	800 per year
4.9 or less	9,150 per day

Source: Global Seismology and Geomagnetism On-line Information System

Director of Utilities

THOMAS G. BRADLEY
SOUTHERN CALIFORNIA
EDISON COMPANY
VENTURA, CALIFORNIA

My job is to supervise the engineering and design of the electrical distribution system that provides electricity to homes, businesses, cities, and amusement parks. I got into this career by chance. I was going to college, and I needed some money during the summer. A friend told me Southern California Edison was looking for part-time meter readers. I got the job and read meters that summer. I really enjoyed it. It paid well, it was outdoors, and it made me realize that I should change my major from commercial art to one of the engineering fields.

My job is different every day. Summertime is busy here because of peak loads and demands due to the heavy use of air conditioning. We monitor the loading on our substations. When the phone rings, it may be a customer complaining or needing some information for a project.

The most interesting project I have worked on was the design of the electrical system that serves Six Flags Magic Mountain in California. It took a couple of years from start to finish before the amusement park was actually opened. They are still adding rides, taking some out, and changing them. The work never stops. There is always some re-designing going on.

Math and engineering are necessary to my work. The science I use most is the electrical theory aspect of physics.

If I were designing a city in earthquake country, I would stay away from natural gas. Fires fed by natural gas were a major problem during the Loma Prieta earthquake.

STUDENT VOICES

I was playing the piano when it started to roll around. My mother told me to run under the table because it was an earthquake, so we dove under the kitchen table.

MANDY HATFIELD
SALINAS, CALIFORNIA

The Mercalli Intensity Scale

Purpose

To use the Mercalli scale to determine earthquake intensity from a set of photographs.

Background

At 15.24 seconds after 5:04 P.M. (PDT) on Tuesday, October 17, 1989, an earthquake with a magnitude of 7.1 occurred in the Santa Cruz Mountains of California. Early readings placed the epicenter at 37 degrees north latitude and 121 degrees west longitude. The quake ruptured a section of the San Andreas Fault and was felt from Los Angeles to Oregon. Commonly called the Loma Prieta earthquake, this was the strongest quake to hit the San Francisco Bay Area since the great earthquake of 1906. Although the shaking lasted about 15 seconds, it killed 62 people, injured 3,757, left over 12,000 homeless, damaged over 2,000 businesses, and resulted in a presidential disaster declaration that covered 10 counties.

It has been ten days since the quake and your company has arranged for you to be part of a team being sent to the San Francisco–Oakland area to evaluate damage done by the Loma Prieta earthquake. Your team is made up of geologists, engineers, insurance adjusters, private contractors, and public-safety officials. For a variety of reasons, all members of the evaluation team have an interest in determining the amount and type of damage and in looking for ways to minimize or prevent similar damage in future earthquakes. The team will use the modified Mercalli intensity scale to evaluate the damage.

Materials

- Modified Mercalli Intensity Scale (Revised) (see page 20)
- Photographs of damage caused by the Loma Prieta earthquake that are shown throughout *Earthquake!*

Procedure

1. Read Modified Mercalli Intensity Scale (Revised) on page 20 and become familiar with the steps on the scale.
2. Use the Mercalli scale to evaluate the damage shown in the photographs of earthquake damage printed in *Earthquake!* Assign each scene an intensity value between I and XII. Record your intensity evaluation on a data table, then select a method to summarize the data as a single score, a range of scores, or another statistical measure that seems appropriate to you.

Design a chart to record Modified Mercalli Intensity (MMI) scores for the photographs of earthquake damage found in *Earthquake!*

Photo Number and Description

- Page 5, left. Pacific Garden Mall, Santa Cruz
- Page 5, right. Pacific Garden Mall, Santa Cruz
- Page 8. House east of Santa Cruz
- Page 12. Marine lab at San Jose State University
- Page 17. Cypress Structure, Highway 880
- Page 22. House near epicenter
- Page 23. San Francisco Marina District
- Page 29. House near epicenter
- Page 40. Highway 1

Highway 1

Technology Education: Earthquake Engineering

Purpose

To design and construct a quarter-inch scale model of a three-story building that could resist earth tremors caused by an earthquake.

Materials

- Materials and supplies given to each group by the teacher

Procedure

Buildings are already built to withstand the downward pull of gravity. But to resist an earthquake, they need to be able to resist sideways (lateral) forces as well. Use the following parameters when designing your model:

1. The structure will be completed in ____ days. (This will be determined by your teacher.)
2. Only the materials supplied may be used.
3. The structure will be three stories tall with a minimum height of 72 feet (scale: 1/4 inch = 1 foot).
4. The structure will not exceed 32 feet in width or depth.

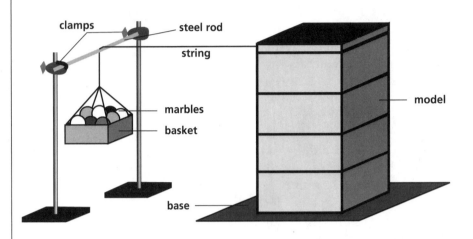

clamps   steel rod
string
marbles
basket
model
base

5. The structure must support ____ of weight (compression) and ____ of weight (laterally).
6. The structure will have a roof.
7. The structure must be secured to a base.

   Build a structure using the materials provided. The diagram shown is a possible model only. The structure will be tested for compression strength and lateral strength. A minimum amount of weight endurance determined by the teacher will be used. Each structure must be able to withstand the minimum amount of weight. Hint: Secure the string to the structure at the same height as the pulley.

Questions

1. What are the strengths and weaknesses of building designs?
2. Discuss how the building designs could be improved.

English: Writing for Personal Expression

Procedure

Now that you have viewed the videotape of the Loma Prieta earthquake and have participated in a discussion about earthquakes, think carefully about your personal reactions as you watched these events. What feelings did you have during the discussion and while watching the news reports? How did the earthquake relate to other events you have experienced in your own life? Write a paragraph in which you explain your previous experiences, personal reactions, and new understandings of the effects of earthquakes.

Use the Peer-Response Form on page 47 and the Proofreading Guidesheet on page 48 as you revise and proofread your work.

Math: How Good Do Your Predictions Have to Be?

Purpose

To determine how reliable predictions of major earthquakes have to be before they should be made public.

Background

The mayor of your city wants to establish an earthquake early-warning system. She has been assured that 72-hour earthquake predictions are currently 50 percent accurate and improving. The mayor is concerned that if an evacuation is announced, but an earthquake fails to occur, citizens will be skeptical when the next evacuation is called. If two false evacuations are called in a row, no one would heed a third call to evacuate.

The mayor knows that 50 percent accuracy is not good enough. But how accurate do the predictions have to be? In other words, what is the chance of two false alarms in a row if the accuracy of prediction improves to 60, 70, 80, or 90 percent?

Materials

- 5 cups
- At least 35 plastic chips of one color and 15 chips of another color
- Optional: materials needed to make spinners

Procedure

You are an expert on probability. You and your colleagues have been hired to investigate the likelihood of falsely predicting an earthquake two times in a row when the accuracy of your prediction model is 90 percent. You are also to investigate the likelihood of two false predictions in a row with models that have 80 percent, 70 percent, 60 percent, and 50 percent reliability. You decide to:

1. Design an experiment using some of the materials listed above.
2. Determine the minimum degree of accuracy that you feel is acceptable.
3. Write a letter to the mayor advising her of your recommendation and giving supporting evidence.

Questions

Think about these questions as you work. Discuss your answers with your group. Be prepared to discuss them with the class.

1. Why are scientists reluctant to publicly announce their earthquake predictions?
2. Are earthquake predictions possible?
3. What would *you* do if there were a 70 percent chance of a magnitude 7.0 (on the Richter scale) earthquake in your area within the next 72 hours?

Writing to Persuade

Purpose
To correlate earthquakes recorded in Maryland with known Maryland faults and then to write a persuasive report in which you defend a site selection.

Materials
- Seismic map of Maryland, page 46
- Earthquakes in Maryland data table, page 45
- Colored pencils

Background
You are the chief executive officer of the Maryland Power and Light Company. You must make the final decision on where in Maryland a nuclear power plant is going to be located. Major requirements for the site are (a) the plant can not be built on a known fault or in an area that has a history of earthquakes, (b) it must be located near a source of water, and (c) it must have minimal impact on the environment. Once you have made your decision, you will write a report persuading state government officials to accept your decision.

Procedure
1. Answer Question 1 below.
2. Determine and label *North* on the map. Identify and label each state.
3. Plot earthquakes that have occurred in Maryland using latitude and longitude to locate the epicenter of each quake. Use a different color for each magnitude. Be sure to include a key to show which color represents each earthquake intensity.
4. Select a location for the nuclear power plant.
5. Answer the remainder of the questions in this section.
6. Organize your information so it will be logical and persuasive. Use a graphic organizer or pre-writing strategy, such as listing or webbing, to organize supporting data, evidence, and logical arguments.
7. Use these ideas to write a rough draft of a persuasive report to the government officials of Maryland defending your selection. Include in your report the reasons for your choice and the facts that support your reasons. Remember to include the evidence you gathered on seismic activity, availability of water, and the impact the plant would have on the environment. Your report should show a clear understanding of the issues and should use clear, correct, persuasive language.
8. Evaluate your report, using the rubric for persuasive writing given to you by your teacher, keeping in mind that you are writing a public report. Then get your peers to evaluate and react to your writing using the Peer-Response Form on page 47.
9. Revise your work, taking into consideration the responses given during the peer evaluation of your writing.
10. Check your work. Proofread it, using the Proofreading Guidesheet on page 48, and prepare a final copy for your teacher.

Questions
1. Using the map on page 46 and the Earthquakes in Maryland data table on page 45, explain how likely it would be for an earthquake to occur in Maryland. Give reasons to support your answer.
2. Does the cluster of earthquakes at 39°50' N and 76°15' W have the same characteristics as those plotted in Maryland? Give examples.
3. Is there a correlation between earthquakes in Maryland and known (exposed) faults? Defend your answer.
4. Having now completed this activity, does your answer to Question 1 change? Why?
5. Use the information on the data table to calculate the average number of years between earthquakes in Maryland. Show your calculations.
6. Make a data table that will show the number of earthquakes by decades (example: 1750s = 1 quake).
7. Graph the earthquakes by decade and answer the following questions:

a. Does the number of earthquakes in Maryland seem to be increasing, decreasing, or remaining constant? Write a brief explanation of your answer using evidence from your data table and graph.

b. When you look at the data by centuries—eighteenth, nineteenth, and twentieth— do you see a pattern in earthquake occurrence? If your answer is yes, describe the pattern and list some reasons that might explain it.

If your answer is no, write a brief paragraph explaining what this tells you about earthquakes.

c. Explain why you think your map may or may not be a good tool for predicting future earthquakes in Maryland.

Earthquakes in Maryland

	Date	Location	Approximate Latitude	Longitude	Estimated Intensity
1	1758 Apr 25	Annapolis	39°00' N	76°30' W	?
2	1828 Feb 24	Bowie	39°05' N	76°45' W	?
3	1876 Jan 30	Annapolis	39°00' N	76°30' W	?
4	1876 Apr 10	Prince Fred.	38°32' N	76°35' W	III
5	1877 Sep 01	Brandywine	38°44' N	76°50' W	III
6	1883 Mar 11	Fallston	39°30' N	76°25' W	IV
7	1883 Mar 12	Fallston	39°30' N	76°25' W	III
8	1902 Mar 10	Union Bridge	39°35' N	77°10' W	III
9	1902 Mar 11	Union Bridge	39°35' N	77°10' W	III
10	1903 Jan 01	Union Bridge	39°35' N	77°10' W	III
11	1903 Jan 01	Union Bridge	39°35' N	77°10' W	II
12	1906 Oct 13	Catonsville	39°15' N	76°43' W	III
13	1910 Jan 24	Westminster	39°35' N	77°00' W	II
14	1910 Apr 24	Catonsville	39°15' N	76°43' W	III
15	1928 Oct 15	Ocean City	38°20' N	75°05' W	IV
16	1930 Nov 01	Round Bay	39°05' N	76°32' W	IV
17	1930 Nov 01	Round Bay	39°05' N	76°32' W	III
18	1939 Jun 22	Phoenix	39°30' N	76°36' W	III
19	1939 Nov 18	Phoenix	39°30' N	76°36' W	IV
20	1939 Nov 26	Phoenix	39°30' N	76°36' W	V
21	1962 Sep 07	Hancock	39°40' N	78°10' W	?
22	1978 Apr 26	Hancock	39°40' N	78°10' W	?
23	1990 Jan 13	Randallstown	39°22' N	76°48' W	V
24	1990 Apr 04	Randallstown	39°22' N	76°48' W	II
25	1991 Sep 28	Randallstown	39°22' N	76°48' W	II

SOURCE: REGER, JAMES P. "EARTHQUAKES IN MARYLAND," MARYLAND GEOLOGICAL SURVEY, 1987.

Note: The latitude and longitude listings above are approximations. For earthquakes 1 through 20, the margin of error is 0.5 to 2.0 degrees. For earthquakes 21 through 25, the margin of error is 0.1 to 0.5 degree.

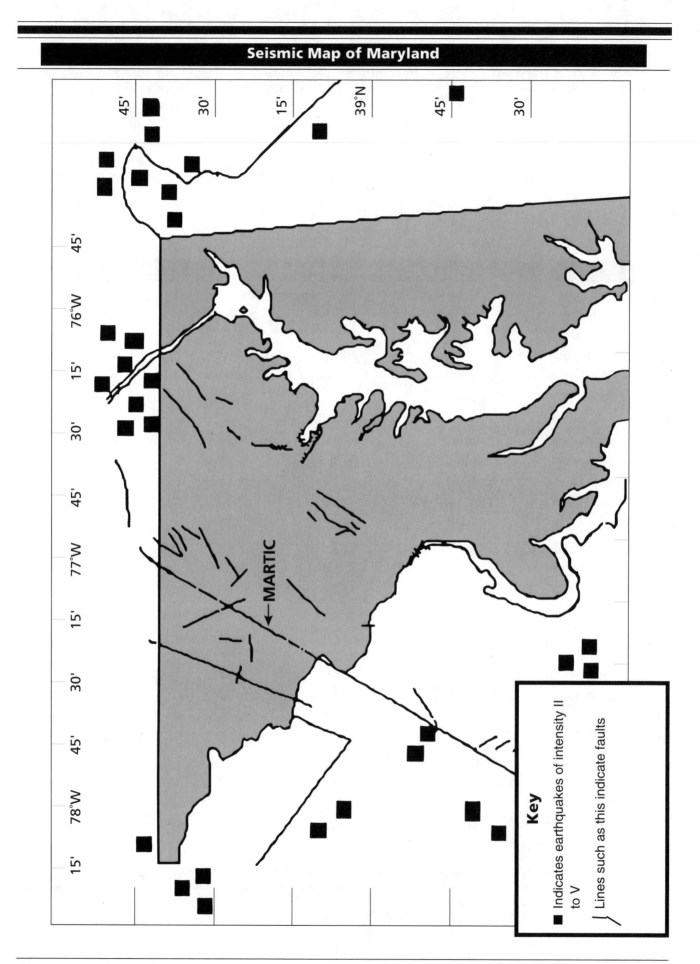

MARTIC

Key

■ Indicates earthquakes of intensity II to V

╲ Lines such as this indicate faults

Peer-Response Form

Directions

1. Ask your partners to listen carefully as you read your rough draft aloud.

2. Ask your partners to help you improve your writing by telling you the answers to the questions below.

3. Jot down notes about what your partners say.

    a. What did you like best about my rough draft?

    b. What did you have the hardest time understanding about my rough draft?

    c. What can you suggest that I do to improve my rough draft?

4. Exchange rough drafts with a partner. In pencil, place a check mark near any mechanical, spelling, or grammatical constructions about which you are uncertain. Return the papers and check your own. Ask your partner for clarification if you do not understand or agree with the comments on your paper. Jot down notes you will want to remember when writing your revision.

Proofreading Guidesheet

1. Have you identified the assigned purpose of the writing assignment and have you accomplished that purpose?

2. Have you written on the assigned topic?

3. Have you identified the assigned form your writing should take and written accordingly?

4. Have you addressed the assigned audience in your writing?

5. Have you used sentences of different lengths and types to make your writing effective?

6. Have you chosen language carefully so the reader understands what you mean?

7. Have you done the following to make your writing clear for someone else to read:

   • used appropriate capitalization?

   • kept pronouns clear?

   • kept verb tense consistent?

   • made sure all words are spelled correctly?

   • used correct punctuation?

   • used complete sentences?

   • made all subjects and verbs agree?

   • organized your ideas into logical paragraphs?

BIBLIOGRAPHY

Arco Editors. *Earth, Sea and Sky.* New York: Arco Publishing, 1984.

Aylesworth, Thomas. *Geological Disasters.* New York: Franklin Watts, 1979.

Bain, Iain. *Mountains and Earth Movements.* New York: Bookwright Press, 1984.

Branley, Franklyn M. *Earthquakes (A Let's-Read-and-Find-Out Science Book for Young Readers).* New York: T. Y. Crowell Junior Books, 1990.

Challand, Helen J. *Earthquakes (A New True Book for Young Readers).* Chicago: Childrens Press, 1982.

Goodman, Billy. Natural *Wonders and Disasters.* Boston: Little, Brown and Company, 1991.

Heppenheimer, T.A. *The Coming Quake: Science and Trembling on the California Earthquake Frontier.* New York: Random House, 1988.

Lambert, David. *Earthquakes (An Easy-Read Fact Book for young readers).* New York: Franklin Watts, 1982.

Salvadori, Mario. *The Art of Construction: Projects and Principles for Beginning Engineers and Architects.* Chicago: Chicago Review Press, 1990.

Simon, Seymour. *Earthquakes.* New York: Morrow Junior Books, 1991.

Tazieff, Haroun. *Earthquake Prediction.* New York: McGraw-Hill, 1992.

Van Rose, Susanna. *Earthquakes.* London, England: Institute of Geological Sciences/Geological Museum, 1983.

Walker, Bryce, and the editors of Time-Life Books. *Earthquake (Planet Earth series).* Alexandria, VA: Time-Life Books, 1982.

ACKNOWLEDGMENTS

Author
Russell G. Wright, with contributions from Leonard David, Barbara Sprungman, and the following teachers:

Richard Chirumbole, West Middle School, Westminster, Maryland
*Vivian H. Clyburn, Herbert Hoover Middle School, Potomac, Maryland
*Nell Jeter, Earle B. Wood Middle School, Rockville, Maryland
*Cynthia Johnson-Cash, Ridgeview Middle School, Gaithersburg, Maryland
*Jeanne S. Klugel, Col. E. Brooke Lee Middle School, Silver Spring, Maryland
*William R. Krayer, Gaithersburg High School, Gaithersburg, Maryland
*Marilyn Matthews, Gaithersburg Intermediate School, Gaithersburg, Maryland
*Carl Merry, Quince Orchard High School, North Potomac, Maryland
*Eugene M. Molesky, Ridgeview Middle School, Gaithersburg, Maryland
*John Senuta, Ridgeview Intermediate School, Gaithersburg, Maryland
*Sheila Shillinger, Montgomery Village Intermediate School, Montgomery Village, Maryland
*J. Martin Smiley, Gaithersburg Intermediate School, Gaithersburg, Maryland
*Clare E. Von Secker, Westland Middle School, Bethesda, Maryland
*Frank S. Weisel, Poolesville Junior/Senior High School, Poolesville, Maryland
Evan Wolff (teacher in training), University of Maryland, College Park, Maryland

Event-Site Support
Nancy Ermoian, Castroville, California

Scientific Reviewers
Paul Spudich, USGS; Herb Meyers, USGS; Caroline Hanson, NCAR; Lowell Whiteside, USGS; David Simpson, IRIS; Ted Habermann, USGS; Diana Todd, NIST

Student Consultants
*Redland Middle School, Rockville, Maryland: Julia Ahn, Amanda Armah, Jerard Barnett, Mark Batipps, Giancarlo Begazo, Twana Brooks, Dean Chilton, Jonathan Codell, Daniel Elbaz, Tim Lewis, Erin McMullen, Kym Thompson

*Ridgeview Intermediate School, Gaithersburg, Maryland: Sean Shillinger, Jeffrey Hsii

Field-Test Teachers
Judith Basile and Karen Shugrue, Agawam Junior High School, Feeding Hills, Massachusetts
David Needham and Gloria Yost, Albert Einstein Middle School, Sacramento, California
Merah Burke, Edmonston-Westside High School, Baltimore, Maryland
Joanne Cannon and Adrianne Criminger, Lanier Middle School, Buford, Georgia
Cheryl Glotfelty and Von Mosser, Northern Middle School, Accident, Maryland
Rodney Clem and Elizabeth McDermott, Southern High School, Baltimore, Maryland
Mark Carlson and Amy Ressler, Westlane Middle School, Indianapolis, Indiana

EBS Advisory Committee
Dr. Eddie Anderson, National Aeronautic and Space Administration
Dr. Lynn Dierking, National Museum of American History
Mr. Bob Dubill, USA Today
Mr. Herbert Freiberger, United States Geological Survey
Ms. Joyce Gross, National Oceanic and Atmospheric Administration
Dr. Harry Herzer, National Aeronautic and Space Administration
Dr. Frank Ireton, American Geophysical Union
*Mr. Bill Krayer, Gaithersburg High School
Dr. Rocky Lopes, American Red Cross
*Dr. Jerry Lynch, John T. Baker Middle School
Ms. Virginia Major, United States Geological Survey
Ms. Marylyn P. MacCabe, Federal Emergency JManagement Agency
Mr. John Ortman, United States Department of Energy
Dr. Noel Raufaste, Jr., National Institute ofStandards and Technology
Dr. Bill Sacco, Trianalytics Corporation
Mr. Ron Slotkin, United States Environmenta Protection Agency

This module began as one of two prototype Event-Based Science units. Successful trials of *Earthquake!* in its earlier versions were instrumental in the evolution of what we now call the EBS model. Charles Doebler, Greg Letterman, and Clarence Wise coauthored the original with Dr. Wright.

*Montgomery County Public Schools, Rockville, MD